I0203712

THIS IS WHAT WE ARE

by

Jack Fenwick

TELEMACHUS PRESS

i

If you purchased this book without a cover you should be aware that this book is stolen property. It was reported as "unsold and destroyed" to the publisher and neither the author nor the publisher has received any payment for this "stripped book."

The names of the characters in this book have been changed to protect their privacy, though some of them may have been given names that are — by pure coincidence — the same as those of several of the people who sit together with us in the stadium. One person has been split into two characters since he didn't want anyone to know that he used to follow association football.

THIS IS WHAT WE ARE

Copyright © 2012 by Jack Fenwick. All rights reserved, including the right to reproduce this book, or portions thereof, in any form. No part of this text may be reproduced, transmitted, downloaded, decompiled, reverse engineered, or stored in or introduced into any information storage and retrieval system, in any form or by any means, whether electronic or mechanical without the express written permission of the author. The scanning, uploading, and distribution of this book via the Internet or via any other means without the permission of the publisher is illegal and punishable by law. Please purchase only authorized electronic editions and do not participate in or encourage electronic piracy of copyrighted materials.

The publisher does not have any control over and does not assume any responsibility for author or third-party websites or their content.

Cover designed by Telemachus Press, LLC

Cover art:
Copyright © ThinkStock/93476855/iStockPhoto
Copyright © ThinkStock/73319401/Digital Vision/Martin Poole
Copyright © ThinkStock/92510509/iStockPhoto

Published by Telemachus Press, LLC
http://www.telemachuspress.com

ISBN: 978-1-938135-12-5 (eBook)
ISBN: 978-1-938135-13-2 (Paperback))

Version 2012.12.22

Printed in the United States of America

10 9 8 7 6 5 4 3 2 1

Reviews for *This Is What We Are*

"This Is What We Are will strike a chord with anyone who has ever fallen hopelessly in love with a club, of whatever sporting creed.

Jack Fenwick takes the reader on an entertaining journey through the sometimes bewildering swings and roundabouts of the Italian rugby scene. We feel his pain when the club he loves ceases to exist and we empathise with him as he tries to make his mind up about the new teams soliciting his affection.

No matter what side of the Great Divide you inhabit, whether rugby union or association football or indeed any other sport, this book will remind you why you sold your soul to the club of your choice, and why all the inevitable lows are necessary so that you can fully enjoy the occasional highs.

Thoroughly recommended, a bonus-point victory for the reader."

Jim Hawker, *The Times*

"A rare and passionate insight into Italian rugby"

Paul Williams, Rugby Blogger for *Rugby World Magazine*,
occasional Red Zone Analyst for BBC Scrum V

"Just read your book this afternoon and it's fantastic! It's a love story written in poetry and I love it."

Gill Paul, novelist, whose most recent book is
Women and Children First

"This book is a thoroughly enjoyable read for anyone who has ever loved sport and really hits home the strange lives that we lead and the measures we go to for love of our team. Like a first love, the team we support whether it is rugby, cricket, football, basketball, handball or tiddlywinks stays with us forever and no matter how hard we try to let go... it always wins us back.

This is What We Are highlights the real heroes of sport: The Fans. Without them sport would be dull and boring and this book eloquently describes the irrational behaviour that supporters go through for the love of their team. A witty, emotional and eye-opening account of what real supporters have to endure for love!"

Barry Irving, former professional rugby fly half
with London Scottish, Glasgow Warriors
and Rugby Parma and Scotland A cap

About the Author

Jack Fenwick was born in Trinidad in the Caribbean, which he — possibly unwisely — decided to leave at the age of one to follow his parents, first to Nigeria and then back home to Britain.

He now lives in Bologna with his Sardinian wife Betta, in less luxury than he would like, and supports one of the rugby teams in the neighbouring city of Parma. He also supports the Italy national rugby team, having lived in Italy for more than half his life and because his wife is his country. And then he supports the British and Irish Lions as well, since — as George Orwell would have it — the red pillar boxes and suet puddings have entered into his soul. Last but not least, he supports the Barbarians because they're everyone's team, and everyone's better for it.

His greatest achievements are having established a good relationship with his wife and dog and acquiring a few friends in life. And finishing this book.

For more information about this book, its author, his blogs and the opportunity to have your own say, visit:

http://www.thisiswhatweare.com

For the Tribes, the Teams ... and 'Jimmy' German Fontana

Many thanks to Nigel, my friend and brother, for his generously-given time, constant encouragement and honest feedback, and to Michael, my best man and editor, for his invaluable painstaking work and many insightful suggestions. And to Olga, for being Olga.

I would also like to thank Telemachus Press for their helpful suggestions and patient support throughout the publication process. I would have aged much faster without you.

Table of Contents

THIS IS WHAT WE ARE

Introduction

Introduction

If you've ever asked yourself why people travel long distances most weekends to watch thirty grown men kicking an oval ball around a muddy field, then this book may just help you get a sense of the lunacy and the brilliance that inspires us.

But — to be honest — if you've ever asked the question, this book is not for you. It's for the people who follow their teams home and away, come rain or shine. For the supporters who help bring about miraculous turnarounds through their efforts in the stands. For whom there aren't important games because every game's important and they've always got to be there. For the men, women and children who turn up week in and week out, as the objects of their affections yo-yo up and down divisions. For supporters of teams who've won everything and of those who've won nothing. For all those who know that, regardless of the size of their trophy cabinet or league position, theirs is the best team in the world and they're the luckiest of supporters.

This is my writing on what we are. It's a series of snapshots, full of zigzags and U-turns and fragments, because our lives are zigzags and U-turns and fragments.

This is my writing on what we are. But it's also my reading of what we are. And others may read that differently.

Seasons in the Sun —
Following Rugby Parma

Cast into limbo

In 2010 Rugby Parma, the team we loved and followed, ran out of money and joined forces with a smaller local club, Rugby Noceto, to place a new team — Crociati — in the Italian top flight. At the same time, two Italian teams — Treviso Rugby and the purpose-formed Aironi, in which Rugby Parma had a 10 per cent stake and which was to represent our region — entered the Magners League, to compete with the cream of Irish, Welsh and Scottish sides. This effectively downgraded the top Italian division, the Super 10, which thereafter became the Campionato di Eccellenza.

We swore we'd never follow Crociati or Aironi.

We thought at first that this was the end of Rugby Parma. But shortly before the beginning of the 2010–11 season, when we were deep in the throes of mourning, they re-appeared, like an unexpected guest at their own funeral, as an amateur team in a regional Serie C league.

They felt like strangers to us.

We'd always said that if you cut us, we'd bleed yellow and blue. And that turned out to be true. But this is how it was in the heady days of the Super 10 and Europe, when Rugby Parma were making waves at home. And occasionally abroad. Before we were cut adrift, in a world turned upside down. This is the way we were.

Men who made a difference

In 1931 three gentlemen from Parma made a trip to Turin, where they met some men from France and England, who invited them to a game. A game played with an egg-shaped ball with an unpredictable bounce. Where the players ran forward but only passed backwards, and where some of them formed a giant tortoise that grunted and heaved. And the gentlemen from Parma said, "That's a good idea!" And when they went home they formed Rugby Parma 1931 F.C. and changed the life of their town. And although we hadn't yet been born, they changed ours too.

Why?

Ask Silvano why he likes rugby and he'll say: "Does the penguin discuss fish? The monkey ask its mate why it likes bananas?" To which the only answer can be: "Well, obviously not. They've got neither the intellect nor the power of speech!" But since we have, could it not be that the question — the one relating to rugby — is worth asking?

What is it we connect with? And do people who don't follow a sports team connect with the same thing in a different way? And if so, how? Or is something missing from our lives? Or from theirs?

The moment

We went to a match and watched them but they weren't our team. We went to more matches and started to shout for them but they still didn't belong to us. And then we bought the shirts, but they still weren't really ours.

Then something happened on the field that changed a game, and something happened inside us that changed us too. And suddenly, they weren't just a team we paid our money to cheer for, but part of us. And those around us in the stand were our people.

No hurry!

There's a big bear of a guy with a beard and kilt among the many London Irish supporters who've come over for the match. Olga wants to have her photo taken with him. They stand in front of me, arms around each other while I rummage in my pockets for new batteries for the camera. I'm getting a bit embarrassed because he probably wants to be in the beer tent with his mates. "Sorry," I say, "I won't be a minute." He looks at Olga and draws her closer. Then back at me. "Take your time!" he says. "Take your time!"

Treviso 35–Rugby Parma 10

It's 28–0 at half-time and Mr Treviso's being nice, and telling Olga how we usually play much better than this. (He's starry-eyed because she was behind the posts when Marcato scored his drop goal for Italy's last-minute win against Scotland.) Slim fountains of yellow and blue attempt to erupt here and there around the stadium when Parma look like doing something, which isn't very often. After an hour it's 35–0. We're being mugged and feel a little peculiar. It finishes 35–10.

Later, at the services, in our Rugby Parma shirts, we feel special and good and joined at the hip.

Rugby Parma 42–Padova 0

Six tries in all and none of them scrummaged over the line. We're free spirits today, painting a glorious picture of the game played in heaven on to a green canvas. This is the game we rarely see but all have in our heads. It's the moment when daily graft and grind unite with sudden inspiration and men create their masterpieces.

We may have beaten Padova today but we would have beaten anyone. We would've beaten you. I could take my season ticket out of my pocket and tear it into shreds, walk out of the stadium and never return.

Rugby Parma 34–Brive 29

Thompson, Goode, Estebanez … we cannot beat Brive. They're will-o'-the-wisps and neck-less monsters. But we will. And we'll do so in style. Today it'll be our turn to be the French team.

When Jimmy drives through their forwards and over the try-line it goes through all of us. So we reach up to the sky and out to our players on the pitch, and out to all of those who've ever worn the yellow and blue on the field or in the stands.

The match report said "1,050 spectators". But there were no spectators.

A bolt to the brain

It's a moment of truth — an instant of realisation. Like meeting your date for the third or fourth time and suddenly knowing you love them because their face has changed.

It's the moment when Andy Goode kneels down near the fifty-metre line in the last minute of the game. He's taking the penalty that'll allow Brive to cut their losses and leave our ground with a losing bonus point — they aren't even attempting to keep possession and go for a converted try. And suddenly we realise we've won. We rise away from our fear and embrace exaltation.

A life-changing game

It's a win that'll make our season, that will stay with us forever. Our little big team with its average attendance of 1,500 have beaten an opponent with crowds and an annual budget seven times as large as theirs. And we always seemed in control. "Remember the Brive match," we'll sometimes say over the next few months, "and never give up."

Olga says it's the best game she's ever seen.

Rugby Parma 29–El Salvador 0

We're playing El Salvador, the Spanish champions, and for once in Europe, we're the 'big' team. They put up a good show but we give them a lesson in rugby.

After the match we meet the team and their supporters in the discotheque that our club's hired and we eat and drink and sing with them. We speak Italian to them and they reply in Spanish, but we all understand one another because we speak the same language. We wish their try had stood, we wish we hadn't nilled them.

They dance with us and give us a lesson in dancing.

The essence

The essence of our love of rugby is the feeling of belonging to a club. Belonging to Rugby Parma. When we watch the world's finest on TV — in a World Cup or Heineken Cup Final — the fact that our team has its place alongside them somewhere in the pyramid of sporting excellence is always at the back of our minds. And when we watch Italy play, we wear our Parma shirts in the stands. Because we know that club supporters are the life-force of the national team. And we're proud to be that.

A conversation on code

The match finished three hours ago and we're still in the beer tent. "Go home!" our fly half shouts at us in mock exasperation. We tell him we are home. He joins in our discussion about the relative merits of football and rugby. I think they're both equally valid. At least I pretend to, since this seems an intelligent thing to say.

"But imagine two cavemen," says Betta, "who see a rock on the ground. One picks it up and tries to do something with it. The other takes a bloody great boot at it. Which of the two is more evolved?" It's a tease, of course. But a good one.

The expat

Alistair phones me from the Isle of Man at the end of every match. I have a whip-round of opinions so I can tell him the right things. I stand at the top of the stadium and speak to him as we salute our players off the field. He's been following the score live on the Net but he wants to know if the match is really over. And I think there's something else. When Alistair calls, he, too, is standing on the steps of the Moletolo, alongside us, with his shirt and his flag.

On the box

We're gathered together in their name at the house of Jean-François, who has the French channels (although he probably shouldn't have), to watch the match at Brive on television. We couldn't go to France because it's a Thursday evening and we all have to work. They show our matches three or four times a season but we've never seen them live before because we've always been at the games.

"Here they come!" I shout, knocking over a beer. And there they are indeed, running on to the pitch in Brive! It's strangely exciting to see them live on TV, and from such a distance.

18

European Challenge Cup 2008–09

We started with a 34–29 home victory over Brive. Our friends in England noticed. We beat the Spanish twice. And came away with two losing bonus points against Newcastle Falcons. We should've won the home game. Could have. Would have. Should have. Newcastle's excuse for their 20–14 'disgrace' in Parma was the muddy pitch. (Oh, for the Geordie climate!) We fought like lions in the last match in Brive. We were leading, and "in the quarter final" sixty minutes into the game, but our legs gave out. Six games, three victories, sixteen points. A great campaign and much better than we'd have put our money on. But it still hurt to go out.

The announcement

We're ten points up at home with two minutes to go. A message starts out over the stadium speaker system: "Now that we're through to the final we'll be laying on transport to Rovigo next week. Coaches will …"

But what coaches will do, we'll find out later, for Giorgio's left us to burst into the announcer's box. There's a live transmission of Giorgio's grapple for the microphone, amid electronic squeaks and squawks. And as the final whistle goes and our players turn to us, with outstretched arms, the system shuts down.

We aren't superstitious, of course. But one never knows.

Failing to make the playoffs

It's the hope that does us in — leaves us as empty as bombed-out buildings. The hope that's become ever dimmer, yet has remained until the dying moments of the regular season, the bonus points here and there fanning the embers of our chances, keeping them alive and sending us running to calculate our permutations after every game.

After we've rescued all that we can, we wait in the Calvisano stadium for news from the Rovigo match, which still hasn't finished. For eight long minutes, the players stand looking at their tribe and the tribe looks back at its players. Eight minutes of belief, anguish and denial. And when the news comes through, we have nothing to say and nowhere to go.

The aftermath

We wander around comatose. We hug our fly half's wife and she starts to cry. The players are on the field, walking about like drunks pretending to be sober, their hands in their hair. The Club President is "Totally gutted. Really, really sorry." Because we'd been everywhere with them and he wanted to take us to Rome.

It's the suddenness of it all. Our season's just … over. We won't see them again for three months now. If we go back home we'll just sit in the dark. So we walk for hours and end up at an American football match.

Yanked into a New World

Now, what the hell was that? When Betta and I leave the stadium
we stare at each other in amazement and laugh for the first time
today. We don't want to say "What a stupid sport!" because it's the
first time we've watched it and we know we aren't qualified to
judge. But what a stupid sport! How can you take a great game like
rugby and do that to it? And why didn't they pass the ball around
more? They all looked top-heavy, like matchstick men, in their
body armour and helmets.

So much for Darwin's theory of evolution!

Scratching the itch

But a nagging doubt's been planted in our minds. It's seriously big in the USA and there must be a reason for that. And not being able to recognise the skills and the strategies rankles. We probably won't be able to close the door on it without knowing what it is we're closing the door on.

So we'll return to the Alfheim Field to watch Bologna Warriors play, to try to get to the bottom of it. After all, our rugby season's over and we've nothing better to do.

It was pretty awful stuff, of course, with strange moves, sacrilegious forward passes and orchestrated applause. And yet ...

Keeping at it

Curiosity pulls us back into the Warriors stadium a week later. But it's like studying Latin at school, where you get the hang of amo, amas, amat and a few declensions and then it's all Greek to you, and you can't see why a table's feminine or there's a vocative case for when you want to speak to it.

We're trying to enter the US but we're continually being denied entry. Because we don't belong here. Rugby Union — like all sports — may throw up occasional gut-wrenching disappointments but at least it's ours. And without homespun broken dreams, what would we be? Nothing, perhaps. Or certainly not living.

Whistling in the wind

The Alfheim Field in Bologna is … well, just a field, with a single 3,000-capacity stand running along one side of it. And we gather it's often pretty full for Warriors matches. On the other side of the pitch, above a bank, there's a railway line and the passing train drivers sometimes sound their whistles as this small-scale, star-spangled stuff shoots past them. It's unfolding before us rather more slowly and we're trying to get into it but, just like the train drivers, we're looking in from the outside.

Roll on the new rugby season!

Blood's thicker

Italy v New Zealand at the San Siro Stadium. It's been billed as "The Sporting Event of the Year" by the media and the sell-out 80,000 crowd will set a new national record for a rugby match. The game against the team that "does that dance" has captured the imagination of the football-watching public too.

In recent years we've been all over Italy with the national team. And abroad, from Murrayfield to Marseille.

"It's not the same though, is it?" Betta says. "I don't feel as though they're mine. Not like Rugby Parma."

And they're not.

Two tribes

Patches of light blue are dotted around the train, travelling to Rome to see the national team. The four Parma supporters are drawn to the red and blue Rovigo shirts. The seven sit down together. The youngest Rovigino wants to study Engineering in Bologna. The women in Parma colours want to know what there is in Rovigo — they've only seen the stadium and ... well, is there anything else? A fourth from Rovigo stayed at home because his dog has died and he didn't feel up to it. Two in yellow and blue know how it is. They sympathise. And they say so.

Faith, hope and fear

Our players tell us they think they can beat Bourgoin next week. And we, who'd thought it impossible, believe them. They'll be playing for themselves, their town and us. And as they stand in the beer tent and tell us they can do it, we're already proud of them. Just for saying it.

Now all week we'll believe they can win, until we cheer them out onto the field, ready to do battle with the giants from the north, and then our fear will undermine our conviction, and desperate hope will take its place.

Rugby Parma 14–Bourgoin 9

Waves of French flair crash against our creaking defence for most of the first thirty minutes, pinning us deep inside our own half. And then, a sudden sucker punch — one dummy, two passes, three players … a seventy-five yard sprint, and a Parma try!

It's like getting the first few numbers in a lottery draw — we're suddenly afraid of what we might lose.

But we just get stronger as, little by little, they fade away. And our drop goal on the hour-mark — its confidence, its poise, its take-that cheek, pushes their heads down. We can see it from the stands. And we know we're going to win.

Accountability

Olga's getting excited about the Heineken Cup Final in Paris in May, for which we all have tickets. I remind her that we might not be going because if Rugby Parma make it to the playoffs this year they'll have the first leg of their semi-final on the same day. Yes, she says, but it'll only be one playoff game, compared to Europe's biggest rugby match. But she knows as well as we do that we just can't go into the Moletolo stadium and tell people we went missing the week before because we were at some game in Paris.

Watching Rugby Parma

When the exile returns, and sees the green fields rising up to meet him, and says: "England, my England" — that's how we feel.
When you get your motor running and the streets smell of coffee and sun, that's how we feel.

When the song builds to a crescendo then comes crashing down like an angry sea against the rocks, and you're sucked up into its soul and taken to a higher plane then spat back down to earth again — that, too, is how we feel.

It's a rainbow of emotions … with holes punched in the sky.

Derby day

Put all the Rugby Parma and Gran Parma supporters together in the stadium, add two teams and sprinkle with a good dose of derby-only fans who come to this game to fuel their sense of rivalry. Then infuse with a dash of magic. This is the Parma derby and it's ours. And more than a match, it's a day. Derby day. And we're all friends in the stands. Though things get kind of heated. But any ire's directed not at one another but at rivals on the field, the referee or fate.

This is the match we cannot lose.

The last derby

No-one said it'd be the last of its kind, before our two clubs joined with others. But we all knew, somehow. And so we gathered one last time in celebration of the city. It was a county fair, with music, food and a post-match lottery for the shirts. Our team's hoops yellow and blue, theirs blue and white. Cut from the same cloth and dyed different colours. It was all us in the first half and all them in the second. We snatched defeat from the jaws of victory. The match finished at nine but many stayed till midnight.

A fine match. A fine advert for the game.

Horses for courses

Some of our rugby friends have become friends in their own right, as it were. We get together with them in the off-season and laugh at their stories about how the official in Africa gave them a dressing down and called them "A very stupid man!" for taking off without clearance, running out of fuel and having to land in a war zone.

But others are friends simply because they love the same team as us and belong to the tribe. And though we like them very much, we only ever see them on match days. Which is strange.

Responsibilities

Matilde's arguing with Silvano, even as he's walking out of the door. Why does he have to go to L'Aquila, a fourteen-hour round trip? He's got responsibilities! She wishes the team would go bankrupt or something and then she wouldn't have to put up with this every weekend. She looks to the women for support, which is strange since they're all decked out in yellow and blue. They make non-committal noises. The men are glad they aren't married to her. The women have thoughts about pain and posteriors.

It's very simple, really. There's a match, Silvano has to be there.

The little things

It's the little things that count. The two guys who sit in front of us, standing up and pointing at their watches as we arrive at the bottom of the stand a few minutes late. The Viadana supporter at the Stade de France hailing us with a cheery "Hey Parma!" after picking out our shirts in the crowd. The "Four beers for the Parma fans!" in the bar at Bath. Our scrum half telling us that he always looks for our shirts as he takes the pitch at away matches. Our players thanking us for our support, though this makes us feel a little guilty because it's us who should be thanking them.

A rugby people

Rovigo's an island of rugby in a nation obsessed with football. A tenth of the town's 50,000 population can be found at big matches. The equivalent of 100,000 in a place like Bristol. We've put them through the mincer a few times over the years, as they have us. In the very last minute of the 2008–09 season they pipped us at the post for a Super 10 semi-final spot. There's what sports commentators would call "an ancient and bitter rivalry" between us. But Rovigo is rugby. New Zealand, Wales, Rovigo.

Europe

Europe. There's nothing quite like it. Massive defeats against the big guns, when we've spent whole games vainly trying to catch the breeze, have been offset by famous victories. Biarritz beat us 7–55 at home, throwing in a few cabrioles and pistolets which had us shouting "You weren't so clever against Stade Français last week!" Unsporting, sure. But nobody likes a show-off. And for every thrashing there have been times when our opponents have drawn the go-to-jail card instead of the five-point gift voucher they expected from an Italian team. "Do not pass go. Do not collect £200."

Fifty matches, thirteen victories, 17–32 average score. Enough said. We're mighty minnows.

Away in Europe

Ryanair to Stansted. Pick up the hire car. Drive to Newcastle in the sleet. Hotel for the night. See the game. Players' lounge — they let us in. Back to Stansted. Bed and Breakfast. Plane home. Job well done. Look at the map. We were there yesterday. Funny old world!

All roads have been honey and rum (though we haven't been taking it on the field). There are the welcomes and questions from the home fans, the drinks together, the handshakes, the thanks-for-comings, meeting the others and setting up camp and flags where our team will notice.

A different breed

Football fans seem to feel a lot of antipathy for rival teams. Particularly local rivals. Joey hates Sunderland. And Roberto doesn't seem to hold Celtic supporters in particularly high esteem. But it's difficult for us to understand why. It's not just a game, to be sure, but we're all part of a great extended family — a happy band of brothers and sisters who seek shelter in the stadium from the alienation of modern life.

We're not into all that negative stuff. We buy into the values of our sport: loyalty, courage, respect and sportsmanship. We don't hate anyone.

(Except Rovigo, of course.)

A chill wind and the spectre of doom

We first got wind of it when we were in Newcastle in 2008, watching Parma play the Falcons in the Challenge Cup. Two years before it happened. Two Italian clubs might be entering the Magners League — the supra-national championship comprising Irish, Scottish and Welsh teams. This idea, greeted enthusiastically by many sections of the press and rugby-watching public in Italy, sent a chill wind whistling through our beer tent.

We worried about our team's future — about an exodus of sponsorship money to a newly perceived 'top flight'. And about a decline in the fortunes and standards of the Super 10.

Times a-changing

We hoped it'd just go away. It didn't. We saw Rovigo supporters waving banners in protest. We loved them for it. Rugby Parma (and others) ran out of money. Rugby Parma joined with Noceto to form Crociati. Our hearts broke. We swore we wouldn't support the new team.

We were told that it would've happened anyway. That it had little to do with Magners League entry and more to do with the recession.

Rugby Parma took a 10 percent stake in the newly formed, purpose-built Italian Magners League 'super team' Aironi Rugby. We vowed not to watch Aironi.

Union with Rugby Noceto

After eighty years, three national championships, three Italian Cups, an Italian Super Cup and fifty matches in Europe, it's come to an end. Or rather, 'a new beginning'. We can forge into the future with a new team, new name, new shirt and new badge. It's time to leave old rivalries aside, for the greater good. The recession, the 'need for reconstruction', the sponsors' exodus with the new Magners League selections, have consigned us to history. But a bright new era for Italian rugby is dawning.

It's a thrust to the heart. We're bleeding yellow and blue.

The Gift of Loss

Looking back

It was after it was gone that we did it justice. That we reached back to the past to celebrate our oneness with our team. To live that unity of purpose and the purpose of that unity with due perception, and feel the worth of half-sung lesser victories, and small achievements, and bitter moments of defeat.

Had it not disappeared, we may never have unearthed it, and if we had not done so, we would never have fully lived it.

Our loss has shown us what we had. And truly given it to us.

My little dog

It was the same for me with Moonie. I used to get back home late, after a day's work and still have to take her out. So I'd sometimes walk through the park complaining, "Come on, Moonie! Get a move on. I'm tired, you know." And at my words, she'd just look up, and wag her little tail and start to dart around, as if to say "Man! Isn't this great?" And when she died, well, I could see I'd been so happy then, of course. But simply hadn't realized.

The best of times are the only times. And Moonie seemed to know that.

Living the Aliens

Observing the wreckage

Aironi Rugby beat Crociati Rugby — the new club formed by the union of Rugby Parma and Rugby Noceto — in a pre-season friendly, and we find ourselves thinking, and saying, that we've lost 19–0. But we didn't recognise our old team in Crociati, didn't feel any sense of belonging, and were only there — sitting under a black cloud of disenchantment and discontent — out of morbid interest, like rubberneckers at a crash scene. Both teams contain strands of Parma's DNA but we aren't going to support either of them. We'd never follow a team built on the bones of Rugby Parma. So why do we keep saying 'we' and 'us' when speaking about Crociati?

First day of the season

We start the season without a team — or at least that's how it feels. This isn't the way it was supposed to happen but it does. We have a hard time at the Crociati match and an even harder one at the Aironi game afterwards. Seeing our former players in different shirts deflates us and leaves us tired and irritable.

At the Aironi Rugby match an old guy, one of the Rugby Parma regulars, speaks for all of us: "We've loved Rugby Parma so much that it's not easy for us to like Crociati. And even harder for us to like this lot."

In the void

We watch Crociati Rugby play Futura Park Roma and think "Who is this team in blue and white?" or "There's Davide. He used to play for us." We sit there in surreal nothingness, watching the players run up and down the field, and listening to the sound of the ball bouncing on the pitch and the players shouting. We clap sometimes because we feel we ought to make an effort. Which is more than we feel later, sitting watching Aironi Rugby. There we feel nothing. Nothing positive, anyway. It's like an out-of-body experience gone wrong.

Kidnapped

Strangely, we all have Aironi season tickets in our pockets and none of us is quite sure why. We sort of bought them by accident. We had our season ticket money and nothing to spend it on, we suppose.

And so we find ourselves standing high up behind the posts at the Zaffanella Stadium in Viadana — where, as things turn out, we'll spend a goodly part of the new season — looking on with detached bemusement and irritation as the tension mounts and another new team, with seven of our former players in their squad, are fanfared onto the field for their first official match.

Michela

Michela doesn't come to either match. When she read the rugby pages she sank into an emptiness, as if she'd lost a brother, as if it were suddenly a different world, and one they'd thrown us out of, without asking and with no warning. She tries to watch the Rovigo match on television but switches off after a few minutes. We feel we have no-one to support and are losing our taste for the sport, our sense of belonging to the game. We're old enough to know that life's unfair. But that doesn't make it feel right.

Hedging his bets

It's the third Crociati Rugby match of the season and the eight Rugby Parma fans are sitting together at the Moletolo stadium. Only one went to the away match near Treviso the week before, doing the 270-mile round trip by motorcycle because his wife had taken the car to visit her sick mother. He says he went not because he supports Crociati Rugby but because he might in the future — you never know what can happen — and then he'd have to have been there. So he didn't want to risk it.

Crociati Rugby 13–Venezia 9

One of the women in our group still chokes up whenever someone mentions Rugby Parma. Another's aching inside. The rest of us still feel slightly numb, but for this match we make a fairly good effort to get behind the players. One of us continues to shout "Parma!" by mistake. We shout half-hearted sporting exhortations of encouragement such as "Dai!", "Forza!" or "Vai ragazzi!" But we can't bring ourselves to shout the name of the new team.

After the match we all hang around the beer tent, chatting to some of the players (though mainly those who used to play for Rugby Parma).

Crociati Rugby 41–L'Aquila 13

The muttering continues but this is Crociati's fifth match and the fourth we seem to have attended, despite our disillusionment. Perhaps we've nowhere else to go on Saturday afternoons. We roll out the same regrets in the clubhouse but they seem more tired and less spontaneous than before. We still can't bring ourselves to shout "Crociati", though it now seems more a matter of principle than something that would stick in our throats. But we applaud heartily, as if the result matters to us. We continue to refer to the team as 'we', speak to the players after the match and congratulate them on the result.

"You shout it first!"

Perhaps it's like the Emperor's new clothes — none of us wants to be the first to shout it. But one day soon one of us will, accidentally, chant the team's name. The finger will pop out of the dyke and a fervent chorus of "Crociati, Crociati!" will come rolling down from our section of the ground.

Some of us still speak about watching other teams instead
(the most desperately unlikely suggestion having been Rovigo) but, well … that's just not going to happen, is it?

Our former captain misses the old club too, but this is where he is now and he's getting on with it!

All we have

And the idea suddenly occurs to me that despite our pledge never to support another team, and what we've told ourselves and one another, we're probably destined to become Crociati Rugby fans. Which is why even Michela came to the last match. Because we're reuniting in the face of the greatest defeat a club can suffer, a battered army of walking wounded, drawn to the remnants of its team and backroom staff, and to the supporters of another club who have experienced the same loss, to attempt to reassemble as best we can and fight another day. And this is all we have.

Our team is dead ...

But we've lost the sense of abandon we had when we woke up on Saturdays with the feeling that it was the first day of a long holiday. When our lives were put on the backburner for a day. When everything else we had to do could go and take a running jump because our team were waiting for us at the Moletolo stadium and nothing else existed. We've grown up suddenly and been plunged into 24/7 normality. Every day's a weekday now. The game we love has become a spectator sport, and we've become spectators.

New World for Old

When San Francisco 49ers play a regular season NFL match against Denver Broncos at Wembley Stadium at the end of October, we're there. We've come to deepen our 'American Football experience'. Though we're doing this in the same spirit that some tourists go sightseeing: La Gioconda — tick; the Eiffel Tower — tick; Champs-Élysées — tick. Paris? Done it!

Eighty-four thousand American football fans from all over Europe have come to get their annual fix of the big time. Pre-match is like a convention. Then Jeff Beck kicks off proceedings with a Hendrix-like version of "God Save the Queen", and some famous American bird treats us to a rendition of "The Star-Spangled Banner".

Why? Why not?

American football's a rock'n'rolling Chevrolet — all sharks' fins and teeth. It's show time, a ceaseless sensory assault with pitch-side action, running deadpan commentary, highlights from other matches shown on the big screen whenever there's a pause in play, and capering cheerleaders. We sit nonplussed and ask ourselves why.

The kick offs are glorious, though — sixty yards flights with a cavalry of charging players. Like the rush of newborn turtles down the beach and into the sea before the gulls can lift them away. Then stop and start, stop and start, until a quarterback launches an impossibly long up-field pass and a receiver catches it and scores a touchdown. And then we think "Yeah! Why not?"

An alien nation

It is like being in certain quarters of Miami, in front of gaudily painted façades of orange, purple and green buildings. Like Disneyland with bells on. We're bewildered by the difference and pleased to be here but we still miss our home. This isn't the America we grew up believing in, which only exists in our minds. It's an America whose glamour prevents it delivering on the excitement it promises, a place where deep emotions are strangled at birth by words that have had their passion scripted out of them. Some people may get it but we still don't. American football's a foreign country.

Resurrection

And then there's the third rugby team we follow, or purport to anyway. The sacred cow — the one we all profess to support. The one exempt from any form of criticism because they wear Rugby Parma's colours, shirt and badge and bear its name. And because they're young and play for nothing.

Just before the season's start, we discovered they'd re-formed Rugby Parma as an amateur team, to play in the Emilia Romagna regional Serie C, the Italian fifth level. We breathed a sigh of relief and said "This is our team!" Though most of us didn't turn up to the first three matches.

Good team, nice team, new team

We don't support Crociati and we don't support Aironi. The team we support is (the new) Rugby Parma 1931, which plays in Serie C. And we don't question whether they're the same team we followed in the past or not. That's a fairly taboo subject. Like the Thing we keep imprisoned in the cupboard below the stairs, which we feed once a day but otherwise ignore. And never, ever mention.

But you'd have to be a reactionary mollusc, clinging desperately to the car crash of your faith, to pretend to yourself that this young team of amateurs is the team we used to love so fervently.

Et tu, Brute?

It's the power of the brand — the name and shirt — that stops us asking sacrilegious questions about Rugby Parma. Though most of us go only occasionally to their matches. And when there's a conflict in the fixture list, some of us watch Crociati while paying lip service to Rugby Parma. This leads, if not to in-fighting amongst our group, at least to barbed in-banter, with Giorgio marching up and down in front of us, like a general inspecting his troops, pointing and shouting: "You! You're betraying your club! And you! A disgrace to the memory of Rugby Parma!" We all laugh, of course. Though some of us rather sheepishly.

Rugby Parma 40–Cesena 11

Respect to the young men who now wear the shirt of Rugby Parma in the new Serie C senior amateur team. They're lambs dressed as lamb and play with a passion and a higher level of skill than we expected in this league.

This is the phoenix risen from the ashes. A phoenix of sorts. A very little phoenix which has just struggled out of its shell and come blinking and stumbling into the world, urged to victory by the cries of sixty diehards standing by an open field, trying to convince themselves that what they had hasn't gone forever.

All things must pass

The post-match trip back home along the dark motorway is an eerie reminder of similar journeys after splendid victories over the cream of the Italian Super 10 or the last stages of return trips from games abroad against top-flight English or French teams. It brings with it the realisation that what we had is gone and is not coming back, or at least not for a very long time. It's true that all good things must come to an end. It's just that you are never ready for your own good things to come to an end.

Singing the yellow and blues

The players have all changed, of course, and we don't know them yet. They're playing with hope for the future, or for love of the game. They aren't playing to live and we don't live to see them play. But we stand by the open field and shout for them. There's no stadium's warm embrace to bind us to the team, but we've ambled happily enough out of the clubhouse past its trophy cabinet and photos of past glories. A victory's no longer a matter of life or death. And there are worse ways to spend a Sunday afternoon.

An arranged marriage

Crociati Rugby … Do we love them? Probably not. It's likely that we're not ready to love again, unconditionally and without reserve.

They've always been 'we', though. Since the pre-season friendlies, we've always said, "We've lost this or won that." So they must be ours to some degree. Or we, despite our lack of feeling for them, must be theirs.

We watch the derby like spectators, with general interest and an analytical eye, and discuss how much we care. Then, when we score a winning try in the dying moments of the match, we're on our feet.

Aironi Rugby matters

A third of the way through the season, Aironi Rugby have lost all their Magners League games and have one hand on the wooden spoon. But this match against Scarlets is different and pulls us up and down like yo-yos. They play their best rugby yet and really look like they're going to win. For the first time — strangely — we're not immune to the result as we look on in desperate anxiety.

Until the last ten minutes when the Welsh run in three tries. Then we all know better than the coach and are never coming back! Until the next time …

The spoils of defeat

Over in the East Stand a group of 500 or so with flags are cheering the team off the field as if they'd just tasted their first victory rather than yet another defeat. They're the Miclas, Aironi Rugby's 'official supporters'. We don't join in, but 'way to go' all the same. When you get behind a team in the bad times they become yours forever.

Our dashed hopes kick off a cycle of irritation that ends in a car-stopping row for two of us on the way home and another throwing his satellite navigator out of the window and having to spend twenty minutes looking for it.

Crociati Rugby v Cavalieri Prato

The young genies from Prato were released some time last season and seemingly can't be pushed back into their bottles. They've no right to play like that at this level. They're first in the table and we've dark-horsed our way into second place, so this is a battle for the top slot. We creep ahead in the fifty-seventh minute and stay there, but despite a try worthy of New Zealand (or our opponents) we're pinned down in our own half for most of the game, hanging on for our lives. Joy says: "This is too exciting for words!"

Our team

It's too exciting for words, perhaps, but not for one word. Or the same word over and over again. Paul starts up the bandwagon with a desperate, angry shout and we all jump on it, as it fires up in synchronous chorus. The bastard child of Rugby Parma and Rugby Noceto — suddenly our bastard child too — is holding out grimly against the odds, and our old hope and anguish are with us again as we will it to victory and the top of the table with cries of "Crociati! Crociati!"

This is our stadium, our team and our town. And you cannot come here and push us around.

No surrender

In part it's probably adversity that draws us in and binds us to the team and one another, at least in this moment. The struggle to win this game against the favourites. The exodus of sponsorship money from clubs outside the Magners League. The now meagre attendances of 400. The fact that next week we're facing Leeds Carnegie, with crowds ten times the size of ours. That despite being bottom of the English Premiership, they'll be taking a win for granted. And that if we somehow prevailed, their supporters would see it as a humiliation for them, rather than a fine achievement by us.

"Sixteenth man, where are you?"

Two years ago, Rugby Parma were averaging around 1,500 supporters per match. There were derbies and other big matches which attracted gates of nearly 4,000. Since Crociati Rugby were formed they've been averaging a mere 340. And they're one of the top six teams in the country. So where have the crowds gone? Well, some are going to Aironi matches instead. Others seem simply to have drifted away from the game. Our coach has written mournfully about low attendances on the club's website and our scrum half tells us it's more difficult to play in front of so few supporters.

Aironi Rugby v Biarritz Olympique Pays Basque

We feel caught between the devil and the deep blue sea. We should know we can't win this one and yet a twelfth consecutive defeat is just too much to contemplate. Winning isn't everything but always losing's disheartening, though it does cement our resolve to dig in deep and get behind this team. It's less that we want to believe, more that we have to. So we take up our positions behind the posts in our smart Aironi jackets — like tribesmen shoehorned into suits who've wandered into the bright lights of the big city — as last season's European Cup finalists take the field.

Flags and fear in the trenches

Our desperation's turned us into flag-waving zealots with the taste
of blood in our mouths, though it smacks mostly of our own as
Biarritz score two tries in the first fifteen minutes to take a 12–3
lead. But Aironi stay in the game with good defence — chipping
away with penalty goals and bursting into life with tries. We're
playing well but the French look better to us, perhaps because we
fear the worst. Losing possession, a penalty and the lead in the
sixty-ninth minute makes Betta shout: "We should write a book
called 'How to lose a match'!"

Vindication

The most beautiful sight in the game must surely be seeing the ball arch between the posts and over the crossbar for a match-winning drop goal in the dying minutes of the match. When it's your team who've kicked it, of course. And especially when you're standing in front of it. And this is what happens. And although a one-point lead with two minutes to go means it still feels like there's a goodly part of a very long afternoon left, the team we've been shouting for hang on in there on to achieve one of the great Heineken Cup upsets.

So how was it for you?

The footballesque scenes of joy at the end of the match would border on the unsporting, were it not for the fact that they're coming from our Davids who, against the odds — 7 to 1, to be precise — have scraped to a famous victory over the Goliaths from the French Top 14. As it is, they're a compliment to our opponents and both they and their supporters are magnanimous in defeat.

For us, Saturday's elation. Sunday's a warm glow. But Monday's just Monday again. Because although it was good — and very good at that — it wasn't Rugby Parma.

Crociati Rugby 6–Leeds Carnegie 44

Big Rugby's arrived again and it's big in all senses — budget, players, steamroller of a team. Our valiant, mainly part-time team fight like cornered wildcats but they're never really in the game. We're now on a par with the English third level and it shows.

As we applaud our team from the field, one of our players — looking like Sylvester the Cat after he's tried to follow Speedy Gonzales all over Mexico, suffering all manner of humiliations in the process — mutters angrily through gritted teeth "It's no bloody fun to go through that!" We shouldn't laugh. But what else can we do?

Little team, big hospitality

But we're proud of our team anyway, and proud of our club's hospitality. The Leeds supporters are served pastries and drinks in their section of the stand throughout the match and plied with sparkling wine and cakes in the beer tent afterwards. They'll later say on message boards that they cannot thank Parma Crociati (sic) enough for their hospitality and that "Sometimes being a Leeds fan is difficult … today was not one of those days."

In the post-match beer tent Phil Thompson seems genuinely impressed with our team's performance. And coming from a World Cup winner, that's enough for us.

An impossible dream

Stade Français de Paris — four times French Champions and twice European Cup finalists in the last eleven years. Just to think of their name's humbling. And yet, on January the 23rd they'll run out onto our Moletolo pitch to face Crociati Rugby in the Challenge Cup. And we'll probably look at one another, shrug our shoulders and laugh nervously. Because we'll know that whatever our team can put on the tracks in front of them, the Parisian train will simply keep on rolling.

Giant-killing dreams don't stretch this far and we're not foolish enough to think they could. Really we aren't …

… and yet …

… it would have given them wings

We can't beat clubs like Stade Français or Leeds Carnegie. It was difficult enough in the past and a fairly rare occurrence, but now it's slipped beyond our grasp. Yet simply playing teams like these stops us being cast adrift, keeps us clinging to the coat tails of top level European rugby. Our Campionato di Eccellenza clubs are sucked along wobbling and out of control in their slipstream, but it stops the gap from widening. We hope …

Crociati Rugby have one objective this year — the Italian Championship. If we could beat the French at home, it'd merely be the icing on the cake — two tons of icing with a cherry on top! But if Nature had wanted pigs to fly …

A conflict of interest

Rugby Parma v Rugby Bolognese is the same day as Rovigo v Crociati and we can't go to both. Giorgio says he'll never betray Rugby Parma and asks us pointedly if that's what we're going to do. I shuffle around guiltily but Betta doesn't. She's going to Rovigo and that's all there is to it — out of solidarity with their supporters, whose team 'have remained true to themselves', battling on in the Campionato di Eccellenza with no stake in the Magners League. And anyway, Rugby Parma in Serie C aren't her old team. We're split fifty-fifty between a team bearing our old name and one containing several of our former players from the glory days.

Decision deferred

We hear — at the last moment as usual — that they're now playing the Parma match the day after the Crociati one. So we end up at both and I don't need to feel sheepish about 'betraying' Rugby Parma. At least not yet. Though we shouldn't be put on the spot like this. It's not our fault there are now three teams. And we're doing our best, drifting dispassionately to see Aironi, Crociati and Parma as often as we can, always fighting a vague sense of distaste, because although the DNA strands of our old team are in all of them, none of them actually is our old team.

Stuck in the middle

If we'd simply been paying clients, purchasing doses of entertainment, we'd now be able just to shrug it off and vote with our feet. "Yes, the craic was good at Rugby Parma and they put on a good show and it was a shame when things changed, but you know things do and now we [insert whatever pathetic thing we do now] instead and that's pretty good too."

But some of us were born with the team when they were born in Parma. And the team was a part of them. And others were born again when they started supporting the team. And it was part of them too.

Market this!

So, you marketing people, downsizers, upsizers and cost-benefit analysts, who sell our banter in the stands and lay rock music behind slowed-down or speeded-up TV highlights, with your talk of entertainment, captive audiences, 'enhanced match-day experiences' and the values of our sport … you know how to sell it but do you really know what it is? You know what works, but do you understand why? You talk about it with authority but can you touch or feel it? Are you really part of it? Do you think you know us? Do you think you're one of us?

A turning point

It'll never be the same. Not for us. For new supporters who strike up relationships with the new teams perhaps. Or for those who took it less seriously. But not for us. We've had our days in the sun, when the boundaries between us and our team were blurred, when we were them and they were us and when loving them was loving ourselves. Aironi are like a national team, that you get behind with everyone else. Crociati are the love child left on our doorstep. And Rugby Parma are a small-scale model of the ship we used to sail in.

Grown up and normal

Perhaps it'll make us more normal ... if people who go to work and follow outside interests, and see going to matches as no more than one of them, are normal. We were like satellites around our team, leaving our orbit for six- or seven- or eight-day forays into the outside world between match days. For an alternative existence where we worked and played and loved, well or badly, in the meantime. Now we're on the outside looking in. The world outside's become the over-riding thing and trips to the stadium are just ... trips to the stadium. And things outside look different. Because they are.

Standing our ground

Rugby Parma beat Bologna in the top of the table clash. But some of us don't feel the same sense of elation we used to when our beloved yellow and blues marked up a victory. We've been relegated four divisions and reduced to amateur status, so a win today's hardly going to make a difference. We're here more on principle, to turn an insolent face to outrageous fortune. During the match we chat about our daily lives and bet on how many people will turn up. Last time it was fifty-eight and two dogs, though one of the dogs left early.

A family affair

The 'crowd' is made up of backroom staff past and present, a goodly number of the players' friends and families, and around a dozen of the old Rugby Parma hardcore support — those who used to attend nearly every match in Italy and abroad. A parent asks us if we "have anyone playing" and I reply "No we don't. We're just supporters. We support Juventus too" — though this isn't true — "and we have no-one playing there either." Betta says this is sarcastic and unfriendly because they're just being sociable. I know this and I'm sorry but it just gets to me.

On to the helter-skelter

Watching Stade Français at the Stade de France must be normal enough, but here in Crociati Rugby's little stadium it's like watching the gods descend to earth. The first third of the game's horribly fascinating as they whirl through our ranks like dervishes and we struggle valorously to plug the gaps and get out of our own twenty-two. If we try to keep possession, they turn us over and if we kick the ball upfield, we don't see it again for a good long time. After twenty-seven minutes it's 3–22 to them. Three tries and a drop. A point every seventy-four seconds.

Reining in the storm

To paraphrase The Killers, "Are they human or are they dancers?" Sitting in the stands we're too overwhelmed by the beauty of their rugby to be shocked. And we're feeling slightly concussed too. So we sit there, bewitched by Stade Français, but occasionally pulling ourselves out of the trance enough to shout encouragement to our lads, although we're generally not connected enough to wonder how it's going to end. It's like watching a film in a foreign language you're not very good at and not being able to quite get your bearings or keep up with what's happening.

But in the thirtieth minute, 'it', as they say in the comic books 'happens!' and pulls us down to earth — a Crociati Rugby try — and a lovely one at that. So it works against them too! Two more penalties in the next thirteen minutes take the score to 14–22 at half-time. And unthinkably, there are only eight points in it.

Relief and disbelief

It can't last, of course, and we know it. The odds were 66 to 1 for a
Crociati victory. The average score so far this season was 45–7 in
favour of French teams against Italian ones in the seven Challenge
Cup games. And there had been no victories by our clubs. So if
someone had offered us, say, a thirty-point defeat before the
match, we'd have grabbed it fairly enthusiastically. As it is, it ends
17–34. Our players have given us more than we could possibly
have asked for and, to be honest, we don't know how. We're
immensely proud of our 17–34 'victory'. And relieved.

A beer tent and rugby people

In the packed beer tent after the match, the Dieux du Stade — away from the field and out of their super-hero costumes — are urbane Clark Kents, humble and courteous, who happily sign autographs while eating, and exchange words with us about Italy, our towns, the way we follow our team. They can't be any different from thousands of other young men all over Europe after a game on a Sunday afternoon.

There's a wonderful mix of players, home-team supporters, opposing fans and star-struck children. And the crowd of 2,400 which almost filled the stadium has filled our day with sunshine.

Forward to the past ...

And here's the thing. When we get up on Monday morning ... and the next day too, there's none of the world-weary, post-rugby fatigue that we've been dragging around with us after our weekend exertions since the start of the season. We feel happy, revitalised and work more energetically. Whatever happened on Sunday to make it so, it was the first match day since Crociati were formed that we lost ourselves in a team, and in the game — that we were as we used to be, when we cheered the yellow and blue of Rugby Parma from the stands.

... and back again

But, we tell ourselves, our growing interest and involvement in all things Crociati in recent weeks, and the warm glow of satisfaction in our honourable defeat against the French, doesn't mean that we've started to love the team or consider them 'ours' in any way. Our support during the Stade Français game was partly the usual Italy v France thing, and partly natural human sympathy for the underdog. And mismatches don't come much greater than that. Which is probably why a Crociati scarf and beanie hat materialised within our group prior to the match. That and, of course, it was a pretty cold day.

'Our team'

Because 'our team' were the players on the pitch, who changed gradually over time as any community changes. It was our name, our shirt, our standing in Italy and abroad, our people in our stands. All these things we recognised as ours. They fostered a sense of belonging in us, a sense of solidarity and common endeavour, of shared involvement, of identity. And because they've all changed so quickly, they don't feel like ours any more and our sense of belonging's fragmented. The glue that held us together has come unstuck.

The retrogrades

We don't travel to Rome for the away game the following week, before the Campionato di Eccellenza is put on hold during the 6 Nations tournament. And when we meet up for the home game against Mogliano a month and a half later, the excitement of the Prato match and the tense challenge of 'Big Rugby' have faded from our minds.

So we sit together and remind ourselves — between loud exhortations to the team and wild celebrations when the final whistle goes — that we don't really care, and that even if we've won today, we won't beat Padova if we play like that.

What's your excuse?

Strangely, this is only the third Rugby Parma Serie C match we'll have been to this season. Something has always inexplicably come up with the others — seemed to get in the way. Perhaps we've been finding reasons not to watch our beloved yellow and blues in such reduced circumstances. Because when we've turned up, an undercurrent of faded glory has left us flat and unfeeling, despite our efforts to talk up the quality of the games, the great day out and our bond with our team. And in their new plain blue shirts, they haven't looked like Rugby Parma.

Something changes

But this time it's different, and whether it's something in the air, something we generate ourselves or a series of mood-enhancing happy coincidences, it's hard to say. But it's certainly a sunny day. And in the pre-match clubhouse, the director of the club thanks us — though we're not sure what for — and pays for our drinks and sandwiches. And when we wander down to the pitch the crowd has swollen, for want of a better word, to over 140. And our team — who we're now starting to recognise — are playing in our traditional yellow and blue hoops.

Closer than we thought

The Italians are amongst the most adaptable, flexible people in the world and some of the best at 'working outside the plan'. Because — well, to be honest — there often isn't one. And for this reason, strange though it may seem, we sometimes don't really know exactly what's going on. And so it is that three months after the start of the season, in response to an off-the-cuff remark to the team coach, we discover that if we top the Emilia Romagna regional Serie C we can, by winning a series of playoffs, bypass Serie C di Eccellenza and go straight into Serie B.

Just like the old days

This startling news — spread quickly around — means that theoretically, at least, it'd be possible to be back in the top flight in four years, rather than the five we'd previously imagined, though this would mean winning every playoff and presumably an interest from somewhere in making the required investments. We're currently third and playing the top team in the league and this information galvanises us, supercharging our exhortations to the team to win the match. Promotion to Serie B — today at least — now feels as important as winning the national championship ever did, as we scrape to a two-point victory.

Aironi redefined

We're in Rome, watching Italy lose to Wales. Aironi have lost nineteen of their twenty matches so far this season in a series of defeats either side of the Biarritz game — each wearing down our exhausted morale. And we've witnessed eight of them from our vantage point high up behind the posts at the Zaffanella Stadium.

At half-time, two young Welsh women, spotting Betta's Aironi jacket, run up to her. "Aironi! Aironi!" they shout in recognition. "We know you. We've been there, with Cardiff. You're great!" Betta says they don't win very often. "It doesn't matter," they insist, "you're still great!" And they're so convinced that we believe them. And that lifts our spirits.

No takers

Betta and I have come down to Rome in a minibus with Olga (who's stopped coming to club matches) and several friends who only go to Italy games. I've been trying to persuade some of them to come to the Aironi fixture against Munster tomorrow, but there aren't any takers.

Italy let a rather sloppy Wales team off the hook and the visitors take control of the game with a clinical drop goal six minutes from time. After the defeat our friends ask "Why did we lose this one?"

"Because you lot don't come to club games!" I reply.

Don't heed the voices

After the long trip to Rome yesterday, I hadn't really been looking forward to another excursion to Viadana to watch Aironi. But I've come because a little voice in my head keeps telling me that things might turn out differently this time. The rest of the gang haven't turned up because they 'need a rest'. Apparently. And I think, that if … just if, we can beat the Irish and end our run of fourteen Magners League defeats, I want to be there. And maybe that'll teach them for staying away. But as it happens, we can't. So it doesn't …

Santa comes to town

It's seven minutes into the second half of an evenly balanced game and we've got a five-yard defensive lineout. But our hooker sends the ball over far too high for our players. It goes straight over them and into the hands of today's lottery winner, a Munster forward, just as a gaping hole opens in front of him in our line. A moment's hesitation — because, let's face it, he's as astonished as we are — and then a quick two-step over our try-line to make it 3–11. And we're going to lose another match we could have won.

Questions

Why am I here? How long can this possibly last? Mustn't every team win sooner or later? Are we close to some sort of world record for consecutive defeats? Perhaps I'm dead and in some kind of rugby purgatory and I just haven't realized it. Or did I commit some crime against Nature — shoot an albatross or something (though I've no recollection of having done so) — and to expiate my sin, will be fated in years to come to wander the land for eternity, accosting fidgety wedding guests and holding them with my glittering eye, while I recount the details of Aironi matches?

We believe

Later, our mirthless answer to the question (asked with much incredulity) "Did you really believe Aironi could beat Munster, twice European Champions, even a Munster sorely depleted by call-ups to the Ireland team?" will be "Yes!"

Yes, because if we've beaten Biarritz we can beat anyone. And yes because we have to believe.

But despite our belief, we're starting to get despondent. We've heard that a monkey in front of a computer with an eternity of time would, by the law of probability, eventually type out the complete works of Shakespeare. But how long's an eternity?

One day ...

Don't the gods of rugby have some sort of ledger in which they chronicle your team's defeats? Well, if they don't, they should. And with it there should be some sort of divine ruling that states that when you get to the bottom of a page, you're automatically entitled to a win.

One day Aironi will win the Magners League and then all the glory hounds who follow only winning teams will turn up at the stadium to watch them. And we'll be able to say we were there through the tough times. If we live that long, of course.

Time without end

There are four and a half minutes left and Italy are leading by a solitary point against France. Olga's staggering around, clutching her chest and fanning herself, like a woman who's just crawled from the wreckage of an air crash, her mouth opening and closing like a landed fish. Beppe's grinding his teeth and spitting venom, his eyes starting from his head. Others are praying or have apparently re-entered their mothers' wombs. People are lurching around, unsure of where to put themselves. None of us believes we'll win — because time might be running out for France, but they're still French!

The soldier

But Betta, with the mental battle scars chiselled into her by the merger of the club she loved with Rugby Noceto, by countless Aironi defeats, by years of last-minute disappointments in the 6 Nations, Italian Super 10 and Magners League, is strangely silent, immobile, outwardly calm. She's gazing into the future as unwaveringly as an artist contemplating the exquisite loneliness of pylons as they stretch over open fields into the horizon, or Wales, or whatever it is that artists contemplate. A little veteran of the trenches readying herself to take another kick in the teeth and to start living for another day.

Who are you?

Betta and I have come to the match in a mini-van with the other seven, who only go to Italy matches. She'll later tell me she doesn't understand them. They're friends and compatriots, but rugby-wise they're not her people. Her people sit behind the posts in Viadana watching Aironi Rugby, or in front of the half-way line in Moletolo, complaining about the union of Rugby Parma with Noceto. These are tourists who like, maybe even love rugby. But scratch the surface and what would you find? She'll say she felt just like them when the final whistle went and Italy had won. But that Aironi beating Biarritz was something else.

Who are they?

None of us understand them really. The tourists, I mean. We're all 'bottom-up' supporters. Our emotions flow up through the Rugby Parma amateur team into one of the city teams, Crociati, and from there into Aironi, which represents two counties, Emilia Romagna and Lombardy. And thereon into the national team. And when Betta's talking to a young Rugby Parma winger, it's just as important to her as meeting Italy's captain. But the tourists aren't even 'top down' supporters. Because they follow the national team but don't seem to have anyone under that. It all just seems to dissipate into nothingness.

"Don't wake us up!"

We knew we'd beat the French one day. We just didn't think it'd be today. And it takes a good while for it to sink in. When people used to ask us if we believed it possible, we always said: "We have to believe!" But whether we did or not was a different matter. It'll slowly dawn on us over the days to come that, no, it wasn't written in stone that France would always win.

For our seven friends it's a famous victory. For Betta, me and the guys back home, it means Aironi Rugby may start winning too.

Being there

It's the eighteenth league game of the season when Aironi finally break their Magners League duck. A 25–13 victory over Connacht — three Aironi tries and a drop goal in a match where the team we're shouting for play good, flowing rugby and the result's never seriously in doubt. It's a good day out and a relief for us. We'd seen this game as the best, and maybe only, chance of a win. They've made history and we've been part of it.

It'll turn out to be their only league win of the season, but who knows what the future holds?

Just the way it is

In the end, though, we still don't see them as 'our team'. Even though we've been to most of their home matches and the away one in Treviso. And we've sat in their colours and cheered them on, had that sinking feeling when things have started to go pear-shaped for them on the field and that sense of anguish when they've been trying to defend a slim lead. But we haven't carried them away inside us when we've left their stadium. They're good guys and we're up for them when they play. But we wouldn't say we support them.

Diversity in the stands

We're not like the Miclas over there in the East Stand, who seem to have unconditionally transposed all their love for their old Viadana team onto this new one, maintaining a constant barrage of chorus and encouragement through occasional thick and rather more frequent thin.

We've got too much respect to barrack the team, and no reason to do so since they're giving their all, and we do get behind them and want them to win. But when we're sitting together behind the posts watching them play, there's a touch of Statler and Waldorf — the two ornery old hecklers from The Muppet Show — about us.

Kith but not kin

There's a lot to like about Aironi Rugby. They're our 'Big Rugby' representatives, playing in a neat little stadium, with some great top level players. They've sort of 'put us on the map'. With an average crowd approaching 3,500 in a 5,500 capacity stadium, there's a good, exciting atmosphere at games. They look after us with good deals on ticket prices and the like and there's good contact between players and supporters. And though the set-up's highly professional, it feels like a club, not like a business. What more could you ask for?

They just don't feel like ours.

"The … gold … is hidden … in … uunh"

So we aren't Crociati Rugby supporters and we aren't Aironi Rugby supporters either. And why not? What is it that creates the bond, that makes you carry a team away inside you when you leave the stadium and keep them with you during the week? Why hasn't the attachment to the shirt that we had with Rugby Parma been rekindled with one of these new teams? Or is it simply a question of time? I don't know the answer to these questions. I can't tell you where the gold is hidden. I can only tell you how it feels.

Carpe diem

Adjusting to the new Rugby Parma side, and their circumstances, has been taking time. It's not like when we watched our team play the cream of Europe. But that doesn't mean it's less fulfilling. Or it probably shouldn't, anyway …

It's like when a partner leaves you, and the next person you meet doesn't play the bass or seem as cool and you can't seem to love them as much. But only because you're seeing them in the context of what you've been used to, which narrows your perspective, blinds you to their beauty. And if we're blinded by the past, how can we live the present?

Winning with kids

Who was it who famously said "You'll never win anything with kids?" Well, the Emilia Romagna regional Serie C Rugby Championship probably wasn't uppermost in their mind when they said it, but it's what our Rugby Parma team add to the trophy cabinet by drawing with Guastalla in front of 150 onlookers. And our reaction suggests that it's as important to us as the League and Cup Double to Manchester United fans.

By playing every match with the innocent fervour of children tearing open their Christmas presents, making each game a spontaneous explosion of exuberance, they've won the league and won us over.

Living the game

When Minnie the Dog goes to the park, her excitement — the way she connects to the experience — makes every time the first time. Her enjoyment never fades. And these young players are the same whenever they take the field. It's chocks away and tally-ho and here's to the game and eternal life. And that's a lesson for living.

They now have a series of knockout games to win to reach Serie B. We won't be going to Bath or Brive, but small towns in other provinces, exploring the vastness of small worlds instead of the smallness of big ones.

Special treatment

As it is, though, they fall at the first hurdle, in the playoff against Firenze, so any further exploration of the vastness of small worlds is put on hold until next season. And we don't seem to mind too much. There's none of the devastation we felt when the old Rugby Parma team failed to win a crucial match, and this team's apparently exempt from the disgruntled comments reserved for Aironi or Crociati. Indeed, we almost fall over one another in our search for positives, deciding it's all for the best — they probably weren't quite ready to go up.

The Emperor's new clothes

Why have we been to more Crociati and Aironi games than Rugby Parma ones when Parma's the team we support? And why are Parma's failures like water off a duck's back to us? These questions were voiced, but only once, and they fell to the beer tent floor, rustled around like leaves in the wind in the awkward silence that ensued, and blew out of the door.

And I'm not going to be the first to think that Parma are no longer our team but simply pleasant young players we're happy to support because they're a flickering reminder of a fire that burned inside us. So …"Go Parma!"

No surrender

Giorgio's the only one of us who's gone to nearly every Rugby Parma match, always giving them precedence over Crociati or Aironi Rugby. And railing at us occasionally for not doing so ourselves. He reminds me of one of those Japanese soldiers they used to find on Pacific islands years after World War II had ended, who refused to surrender or believe it was over.

The rest of us probably just aren't used to Serie C. It's the bread and butter of Italian rugby, and we respect it for that. And of course it's not that we've ever had the haute cuisine of the French Top 14 or the English Premiership. But we'd grown used to the good, honest meat and two veg of the Italian Super 10 and the sudden change of diet's difficult to digest.

A glass half-full

We're now part of a regional rugby pyramid rather than supporters of a single club. So we get together with fans of other clubs with whom we wouldn't previously have formed such close relationships. Noceto fans — who've suffered a similar loss to us — cheer Crociati Rugby alongside us at the Moletolo stadium. And GranDucato Parma — the result of another union between clubs — are Crociati's new local rivals. But their fans also support Aironi. So we're cheering for different teams when they play Crociati but for the same one at Aironi games. And this kind of reminds us we're all the same.

The wake-up call

There's news of another change on the cards — this time Crociati joining with their new local rivals GranDucato Parma, themselves the product of a recent fusion. It fast-tracks us through an emotional labyrinth of rapid soul-searching, from which we emerge, blinking at the sunlight, dazzled by the realisation that it no longer matters to us. Our old team was a faith, something we carried around inside us most of the time. And it now seems to us that by following Crociati we were simply being institutionally religious, doing what was expected of us as supporters of one of the two clubs that came together.

"Blow, winds, and crack your cheeks! … Oh, alright then, don't!"

Realising we don't care if Crociati Rugby and GranDucato come together is like a bucket of cold water. Like struggling in the centre of a tempest before scene-shifters come on and move the backdrop and switch off the snow machines and you realise it was only a stage set. And there's suddenly silence, broken only by the clinks and clunks of people packing things away. So you just get your coat and go home.

But are you serious?

So the news of the new merger — or whatever it'll be — doesn't hit us in our collective solar-plexus like the demise of our top-flight Rugby Parma team had done. And that's a sign that we really didn't care about Crociati after all. But it does seem as if we're being messed about a bit. We've spent a fair amount of money and energy not caring about a team and we'd at least like the option of continuing not to care.

And anyway it's just depressing, this constant shifting of sands. And if they think we're going to bother not giving a damn about yet another new team, they're sorely mistaken.

What's it all about?

So what was the point of turning up to nearly every match to watch the team struggle into a semi-final playoff position if they're not going to be around next year? What would winning the Italian Championship mean if they aren't around to defend it next season? And what is it with all these fusions? Crociati Rugby were formed from two different teams and GranDucato from three. And now these two are joining together. If it goes on like this, we'll end up with just one team in the whole country, playing against itself. We just aren't interested any more!

Seeing it out

Not being interested doesn't stop us turning up for the home leg of
the semi-final against Rovigo, where they let us in free as a sign of
solidarity, though Lord knows they could do with our twenty euros.
And even though we lose and it's extremely improbable we can
reverse things in Rovigo, it doesn't stop Betta and me travelling
there the week after, waving our Crociati scarf when the final
whistle's gone and we've once again been beaten, and arguing over
nothing in the car back home. "Lucky for us they're not our team!"
Betta will later say morosely.

The smoke clears

It's two years after our first American football match and we're back at the Alfheim Field watching Bologna Warriors again. Suddenly the scales fall from our eyes and we just 'get it'. And strangely, it happens to both of us, Betta and me, at the same time. It's like that trick picture where you can see only the pretty young woman or the hag. And then everything comes into focus and you can see them both and mentally flick from one to the other at will. We get the skilful runs into space, the passing and the kicking, and the teenage cheerleaders, the band that starts up during breaks in play and the orchestrated cheering. And though we're still visitors, it sure seems good.

The mind boggles

Four well-dressed young men in their early twenties are passing the Alfheim Field as the players warm up on the pitch.

"What's going on there?" one asks the others. And they stop to look inside the stadium. "It's a game of rugby," one of them eventually says. And, satisfied with that reply, they're on their way.

We look at one another nonplussed. This is typical of a country where 'sport' is a synonym for association football. I want to shout after them: "In Australia or France, even a ninety-year-old grandmother who never watches sport knows the difference between rugby and American football!"

But I don't, of course.

Home and away

The Superbowl final featuring Bologna Warriors against Parma Panthers has been fixed for the Moletolo stadium in Parma of all places. Betta and I hadn't kept our eyes on the fixture list or planned for it, so we booked a holiday for the same time. At first we're sorely disappointed to miss the final at 'our rugby stadium'. But then decide it's all for the best. It'd feel too strange to turn up in Parma and cheer for the 'away team'.

We tell our Warriors supporter friends, from Bologna, where we also live, that they're going to our spiritual home and to please kiss the ground for us as they enter.

The learning

So what have we got out of it so far? We've learned that the proof of the pudding isn't simply in the eating but in eating enough. That American football's as good a sport as any, including rugby union. Not to us, perhaps, but objectively speaking. That it's horses for courses and we're fundamentally all the same. That a tribe's a tribe and there's no excuse for ignorance. That it's never too late to learn. That it, too, is about skill, strategy, sporting values and community. It's enlarged our world and given us culture. Men in armour, we salute you.

A twist of fate

And if we hadn't stumbled out of the Centro Sportivo San Michele in Calvisano on the 9th May 2009, feeling concussed and sick at heart at Rugby Parma's last-minute failure to make the playoffs, we wouldn't have fallen into an American football match by chance, after hours of aimless meandering, or been set on a path of discovery which, through the people we've met and the understanding we've gained, has enriched our lives. If we could travel back to the past and change things, we'd still take the playoffs, of course. But you have to count the positives.

A detached attachment

We're still outsiders, of course, though now appreciative ones. We can share in the culture, appreciate the differences — reach into a different world. But we're merely revolving around it, not moving around inside. It doesn't enter our souls. Though we wear Warriors caps and shout exhortations to the team, inside we're quite relaxed at the Alfheim Field. There's none of the anguish or exhilaration we feel at the rugby. It's three hours of detachment, of observation, of relating to other people as relative bystanders. Though when people ask us if we understand the game, we're proud to say yes.

The tourists' viewpoint

The tourists — our friends who only go to international matches — are surprised when I say I won't follow any team that comes out of a union between Crociati Rugby and GranDucato Parma. But surely, they say, it's better for 'rugby in Italy'. A stronger Parma team means a stronger feeder team for Aironi Rugby. And a stronger Aironi side means a better national one. They're voicing the opinion of many professional commentators who see the good of the national team as the be all and end all of everything. But the cookie doesn't crumble like that — not for us in any case. I feel like saying "Well, why don't you go and see them play, then?"

It's only natural

The tourists love their country but most would put their city first. And they'd put their families before their cities. And that seems natural enough. But it's the same for us rugby-wise. They're consumers who buy rugby as a product. (And nothing wrong with that, of course.) But we're supporters, and because the club game's the bread and butter of Italian rugby and the bread and butter that feeds our identities as rugby people, even though we support the national team, we just can't put them first in our hearts. And that seems normal to us …

Much ado about nothing?

Now you could be thinking "What's the big deal? So their club had to merge with another one! They should just get a grip and try and bond with the new team. And if they can't do that, they should spend their weekends at the American football instead, or down at the bar of the girl with the Maori tattoo who rides a Ducati."

But things aren't that simple — and we wouldn't be supporters if they were. Though having got this far in the book, you probably knew that already.

'Project Parma' bites the dust

And then, just as suddenly, the amalgamation of the Parma teams is put on hold. GranDucato sells its 'sporting rights' to Reggio Emilia who, although failing to gain promotion by winning the Serie A playoff, thus take GranDucato's place in the Italian top flight. And Rugby Parma pull out of Crociati, leaving Noceto as the sole stakeholder in the team we've been following. So there's nothing of our beloved yellow and blues left in Crociati, except some former players and the newly appointed coach (who we'll always love from his playing days at Rugby Parma).

On-off, on-off. Italy's the on-off country.

Too tired to fight it

Some, including a few of the Crociati backroom staff who had originally come from Noceto, assume that we, the former Parma hardcore support, will just give up on them. But what can we say? We're too weary of the changes to think about it any more. Just give us whatever team's around and we'll troop into the stadium, the only thing that still feels like ours. If there's a team there that plays rugby and the price is right we'll just come, okay?

And so it is that at the start of the 2011–12 season, we add Crociati season tickets to the Aironi ones we'd accidentally renewed.

Never say 'never'

If you'd told us two years ago that we'd be turning up to watch a team wholly owned by Rugby Noceto (who?), we'd have laughed in your face. Among the reactions we considered to the union of Rugby Parma with Noceto were:

Never following a team built on the blood of Rugby Parma

Stopping going to games completely

Telling Aironi and the Magners League to go and do something to themselves that can't be explained politely

Publicly burning our shirts in protest (though we'd have had to buy new ones)

Which just goes to show you never know what you might do. Though this doesn't mean we're Crociati supporters.

Non-supporters

A profiler's nightmare

Someone once said that there are three You's. There's the You you think you are, the You that others think you are and the You you really are. If this is true I can't really say with any certainty who we are. I can tell you, however, what we say we aren't and that's Crociati Rugby supporters. Now this might seem strange since we went to most of the Crociati games last season and have season tickets for this one, shout "Crociati! Crociati!" while they're playing, send one another emails with the latest club news and say 'we' and 'us' when referring to them.

A canard

And some might suppose that if it walks like a duck and talks like a duck, it must be a duck, but the world is vast and the world is strange and you can never set too much store by appearances. Though any misconceptions about where our loyalties lie must be shared by the club, because before the Stade Français match last season they gave four of us free passes to the remaining games for being "such great supporters". Not that anyone clarified matters by refusing them or saying things like: "Oh no! I couldn't possibly … I'm not a supporter, you know."

Curiouser and curiouser

So in this funny old world you get Inter or Milan supporters who never go to matches and non-Crociati supporters who spend half their lives either camped out at the Moletolo stadium or sending one another emails about how the club that isn't theirs is doing.

And we aren't Aironi Rugby supporters either. And this seems more obvious since, although we've accidentally bought Aironi season tickets two years running, we've only ever attended the home games ... except for the Treviso match, of course. But we don't send emails about them to one another and only say 'we' or 'us' while we're at their stadium, which we keep threatening not to go back to.

Giving them the bird

Giorgio might have more credibility as a non-Crociati supporter
than the rest of us, at least in the eyes of those who think that it has
to walk like a duck and talk like a duck to actually be a duck. That's
because although he does attend Crociati matches, he spends a
great deal of time railing against them, shouting "Noceto!" at them
and generally being grumpy and malcontent. And we love him for
that, of course. There's just the small fact that he attended almost
all their matches last season, which might lead some to suspect that
he isn't entirely devoid of duck-like attributes.

Part of the system

Giorgio probably took the demise of Rugby Parma harder than anyone. Only illness would keep him away from their matches, home or away, in Italy or abroad. He refuses to recognize Crociati Rugby as his Parma team, insisting on calling them Noceto. But even Giorgio is part of 'the system'. He comes to Crociati Rugby games when the amateur Parma team aren't playing. In one breath he calls them Noceto and in the next he'll say to us "Hey! Won't it be ironic if we win the Championship with Crociati when we never managed it with Rugby Parma?"

Till the next time

And if you've read the book this far, the chances are we're just the same as you. And perhaps one day we'll meet at the Moletolo stadium in Parma, or the Stadio Zaffanella in Viadana, where Aironi play. Or we may bump into one another in Edinburgh, Dublin or London. And though we still support the Italy team, it's unlikely we'll meet you at a 6 Nations match. For nowadays we're too busy not supporting Crociati and Aironi to make it to Rome.

And if you see us, say hello, for though we won't have met, we'll feel we already know you.

Our Jimmy

Who is 'Jimmy' German Fontana?

He was 'Our Jimmy' both on the field and in the beer tent. The world's number one loose-head prop. Not the best, perhaps, but unquestionably the greatest. He made us feel that life was just a game, and we were all involved in it.

His speech at Rugby Parma's 2009 pre-season presentation to the town was seven words long. He took the floor, pointed at us and said "I just want to thank that lot!" then sat down again.

He left the team when it broke up at the end of the 2009–10 season. Like all of them. But he's still 'Our Jimmy'.

Every team's supporters have their Jimmy Fontana. And ours was Jimmy Fontana.

The Girl with the Maori Tattoo

The girl with the Maori tattoo

The girl with the Maori tattoo runs a little bar a couple of streets away from where I live, which often turns out to be on my way to wherever it is I happen to be going, for some reason. I asked her if it was because she liked rugby but she said no — she was just cool. She rides a yellow Ducati and I occasionally see her flinging it around town. And sometimes, when I'm feeling down about the demise of my team, I think of this. And the Italy women's rugby team. And life suddenly seems a bit rosier.

Reflections from an Oval World

Inside out and outside in

Some of these reflections were written when we followed Rugby Parma in the Italian top flight. When I was on the inside looking out. When the world was simple and there was nothing to question. Others were written after the demise of our team. When I was on the outside looking in. Looking in at supporters of other clubs whose lives hadn't changed.

Just what we do

We go to around 85 per cent of our team's matches every season. Only illness or work will keep us away. It's a duty (and an honour) to follow them, as well as a pleasure and 'just what we do'. If one of our spouses is ill they'll tell us they can look after themselves and not to worry about them — just to get off to the match, because the team need us. We'd never boo our players for not playing well — it'd go against the social contract we have with them. And in any case, we wouldn't want to.

The cycle

By Saturday that small spark of anticipation at the back of your head has become a slow sunrise filling your mind, brightening everything with the rays of match day. On with the shirt and off to the stadium.

Tension, focus, release and celebration. Or post-mortem. "What if ...?", "We could still ..." and "This doesn't mean ..." You talk to yourself as much as to the others.

Then home. Off with the shirt. Empty your mind and collapse on the sofa as tired as if you'd played yourself. And wait to come down. Tomorrow you'll be normal again.

Match day

From the top of the approach road you can see, half-way down, the arches of the two stands that flank the pitch and little groups of supporters approaching from each end, like iron filings attracted towards the poles of a magnet. They'll meet in the middle, at the entrance to this hub of yellow and blue fervour. They're united and happy. There are no captains or kings under this shirt, nobody to look down on you, or up to you. There are children, teenagers, young and older adults, and senior citizens, but today they are all young.

The flight

It's the take-off that's the most exciting part: the release of the week's tensions after that sudden rush of blood as the players take the field and the teams line up in front of you.

Sometimes the flight is smooth and fast and you wish it would last longer. More often, there's turbulence, and the palms of your hands are moist and you want it to end. But end safely. You vow that if all goes well, you'll no longer worry about those little things, for your priorities have been readjusted. And you promise that if you get down safely, you will be good.

Time

Time is relative. That we know. And we didn't need Albert Einstein to tell us, for we feel it most weekends. Sometimes it's like an episode of The Outer Limits, where time has almost stopped. The seconds stretch out as if they are elastic and only when both you and they are at breaking point does it happen … clunk … another minute passes on the stadium clock. But sometimes it's like a Benny Hill chase. The world has sped up and you can't get off. And it can change from one to the other in the blink of a try.

Why do we love them?

The love for our team spans age, language, culture, social position and job description.

And what do we love them for? We love them for the spaces between what they are and what they want to be, which are the spaces between what we are and what we want to be. Because they are trying to carry our flag up that great steep hill and plant it at the top. Because when they cross the line they've crossed all our lines for all of us. And when they fail to cross the line, we love them for their struggle.

The shirt

The site of the shirt unlocks feelings of exquisite pleasure, transporting you back to good times spent together, memorable trips abroad, the fuel of victory and the comradeship of defeat. It plugs you into the power of passion and the timelessness of community.

The shirt itself has magical properties, of course. It multiplies in ever-increasing concentric circles, to spread a carpet across another team's stadium. It can get you on television at live matches. It elicits drink and conversation from strangers. It makes your team appear more skilful than they really are, and more deserving of reward than their opponents.

This is who we are

We are the advance party. We are here in your town in our uniforms of yellow and blue preparing for battle. We are coming to destroy you, to plunder your fields and silence your songs and take our booty back home. This is who we are.

We are the advance party. We are civilised and modern and reconstructed. We are here in your town in our uniforms of yellow and blue to extend the hand of friendship, to discover who you are and what you do. To admire your diversity and enjoy our communality. And this is who we are.

The tribe

At one level what goes on in front of us on the pitch is just a game. But when we unite to watch our team, we go back to where we came from. And we chant to fill that place with life. Or to bring about victories, or offer them up. And if we lose, we chant to summon the spirit of victory for the next challenge, or to silence the silence within us.

Or perhaps it is always to silence the silence within us.

Not fun

Betta stares in stunned amazement at Enzo, who's just suggested that match day must be 'a fun day out'. It's like summing up life itself as simply 'fun'. And it's so much less and more than this. It's a weekly reunion of like-minded people, some on a mission. It's a pre-match homecoming followed by ninety minutes of tension, agony, explosions of joy and implosions of misery, while the world outside has stopped. It's the rebuilding of belief in the post-match beer tent after a defeat, where negative comments fish hopefully for optimistic predictions for the future.

Follow follow

It's a quest for those moments of divine synchronicity, on the field and in the stands, when spirit and instinct transcend conscious thought and take us to a higher plane of existence, which is just as real as the rest of our lives. It's all of us, moving together, searching for sustenance, for new frontiers, for a place to call home and for one another. It's a part of ourselves that we return to, for this is what we were and this is what we are. It's not entertainment. It is much, much more than that.

Something else

Entertainment, we imagine, is watching a film in an air-conditioned cinema in well-padded seats with a Coke and popcorn, or playing crazy golf or something. But watching your team battle it out on the field is an often uncomfortable experience involving high levels of stress and a longing for the final whistle. And this doesn't mean that it's not worthwhile. After all, Man has always expended copious amounts of mental energy that take him out of his comfort zone, in pursuit of the things he loves. It simply means it's not entertainment — it's something else.

Missing the point … again!

A former association football player turned pundit and sports journalist, writing in The Times, is the latest proponent of the Great Fallacy: "When it comes down to it," he says, "football is entertainment, like going to the cinema …" But no Liverpool supporter would fly to Istanbul to see a movie. They wouldn't feel devastated if a film didn't end the way they wanted. And they'd always take an ugly, turgid win over a beautifully played out, exciting defeat.

Supporters aren't merely clients who demand to be entertained. And their players aren't performing fleas whose job it is to dance for them.

Enjoyment

We're watching Newcastle United play Manchester United on TV. A good match — skilful, exciting, close. In the second half the commentator remarks that it's a great game and the supporters are enjoying themselves immensely.

But who can he possibly be talking about — a few neutral observers in the crowd?

The faces of the two team coaches during the match have shown focus, concentration, tension, worry. Fleeting signs of joy, anger and frustration. One of them will no doubt enjoy his victory after the game but they haven't been 'enjoying themselves' up to now. And it's no different for the supporters.

Fangeist

There's something else at the ground and it's alive. A mantle of energy that cloaks the stadium and feeds off our emotions. It enters our minds, shielding our thoughts from the world outside and directing them to events on the field. We're its appendages. It twists us this way and that and draws us together. It has no morals, no sense of right or wrong, is red of tooth and claw. We surrender our egos, our self-determinism and our sense of logic, and let it take us on its roller-coaster ride.

The puppeteers

The gods of rugby pull on our strings as if we are marionettes, with a limited but well-synchronised repertoire. There's the move where we all jump up with our arms in the air. And there's another where we slump in our seats, with our heads in our hands. A difficult one to pull off must be the clenched fists to mouths, and the false-start half-leap in the air can't be easy. And they sometimes have a laugh too — when some of them pull all their strings together, as hard as they can, while others let theirs go.

Part of the crowd

We flow in and out of the crowd, sometimes towards our own little group, and sometimes away from the stand to take our places alongside the players on the pitch. This isn't a thronging big city rush-hour pavement, where you're physically but not mentally part of the crowd, but a source of energy which we feed off and into, which lets us each drift away and pulls us back together again. Sometimes we just draw into ourselves, in foetal positions, or on walks of solitary suffering, cursing our team for its errors or counting the positives.

The sixteenth man

There's a self-perpetuating virtuous cycle of vital energy that flows from the stands to the team on the field and back again.

At home we make up most of the crowd. Away, we're a small presence in a foreign field. But they know we'll be there, and some of them look for us to get their bearings when they run out on the pitch, before sealing themselves off inside the bubble of the game.

We're the sixteenth man. We call the tune and dance to it too. We're the puppets and the puppet-masters. Just like our team.

A different perspective

If we watch the match later, on television, it can seem quite different. We may not have been pinned down in our own half for most of the game after all — we might even have looked the better side. And perhaps, seeing it again like this, we weren't so lucky to win. Or maybe our opponents played better than we thought at the time.

Perhaps it's knowing the outcome that makes the difference — our minds are unclouded by elation, disappointment or anxiety. Though sometimes, when later watching our kicker miss that match-winning penalty on the screen, we still can't help hoping it'll somehow go over this time.

Tricks of the mind

When we look back at the sports reports, we see it's not true that almost every win hung in the balance. That our team had us writhing on tenterhooks for an eternity before kicking the ball desperately out of play in the eightieth minute to emerge victorious. That every match was a long, drawn-out affliction akin to crawling over broken glass. In the same way you really don't always choose the slowest-moving queue in the bank, even if it seems that way. It's just that those are the times that stick in your mind.

Future perfect

We don't live for the present when we watch them. We live for the past we hope it will become. We don't want to be winning — we want to have won. Our team is what they've achieved in the past. Twenty years ago, or twenty seconds after the final whistle's gone. It's not like special moments with the one you love, or breathing in Nature on a mountain hike, when you wish it could last forever. We want it to end, if we're winning. Because our team is what it's done. And what it will have done, when the future becomes the past.

Living the past

So, as supporters, we don't live in the present. Unless we're sailing plainly along with nothing at risk, when we can sit back in the sun. But if we're not, it's not like special moments you wish could last forever. Those last minutes of the games as we edge … well, we wouldn't want to live like that all the time, though we couldn't live without it.

And our team, too, don't exist in the present. They're not what they can do today. For truth be told, we don't know what they can do today. We can only presume it. From what they did yesterday.

It's what we've done that makes us what we are. And it's the same for our team.

It's all relative

When you're middle-aged and you're no longer going to live forever, and you're not going to learn how to fly, you might sometimes think about the relatively short time you have left. By the law of averages, thirty odd years. Doesn't seem that much, does it?

But think instead about the long close season: you have another thirty of those to get through. Works for us — pulls us out of the shadows a bit.

Plus on est de fous …

On a wintry Friday morning in December 2010, with snow causing travel chaos over most of Europe, 400 men, women and children in their tribal finery — some as young as four — leave the Home Counties and begin to run the gauntlet of cancelled trains, coaches and planes and sub-zero temperatures, all in a bid to watch their team run out onto a pitch in south-west France on the afternoon of the next day.

Of the 250 who make it, a good few are still stranded in Nice sixty hours later. They're all plain bonkers, of course. But who in their right mind wouldn't be?

They're at it again!

In the end they all make it back, though when had been a secondary consideration, flung far into the dim and distant future by the challenge of getting to the game by 4.30pm on the Saturday.

No sooner have they returned than they're posting on their message boards, making plans for a trip to Ireland for another match in January.

When asked to explain this wonderful madness they say they've got more money than sense ... and not a lot of that!

Part of the show

They aren't spectators. This green and black and white army stuck between trains in freezing railway stations or sleeping on airport terminal floors with their flags and their banners, taking in and adding to the sights, the sounds and the smells of the places in which they encamp. They're part of the show. The show of life.

Winning memories

A great win — particularly one over a bigger and better team — can set us up for weeks. It fills us with positive energy that flows into our work and personal lives. And then it takes its place in the archive of our memories, to be rolled out and relived over the years in the beer tent. We can still feel the exhilaration of formidable achievements long after heart-rending failures have faded into the background and lost their sting. But the disappointments we share, strengthening the ties that bind us to our team, do not stay with us. Our memories are only good.

L'entente cordiale

Françoise and Claude have fond memories of the 2007 Heineken Cup quarter final between Leicester Tigers and Stade Français at Welford Road. They'd ordered their tickets directly from Leicester and were seated amongst all the Tigers fans, while most of their compatriots were on the other side of the ground. When they got to their seats the Leicester supporters stood up and shook their hands warmly. They bought them beers at half-time. And as they left they formed a queue to say "Goodbye and thanks for coming!" The last to do so was very young and a little shy about it.

Baa-Baas

Barbarians!

Betta and I still have the Barbarians — now our favourite form of transport. When they appear before us we're pitchforked into a past — real or imagined — where sport was pure abandon, where swashbuckling heroes, unfettered by fear of failure, stirred up a maelstrom of boundary-pushing skills on the field, for pure love of the game.

And they still play like that today. Their wild insouciance gives us a liberating dose of the are-they-really-trying-to-do-that heebie jeebies, but makes us feel good and sets us free. Because they really are trying to do that and 'that' is the whole point of the Barbarians.

The legacy

And so they take us back to our youth. To when we too cocked a snook at what was safe and sensible. To parents speaking in awe and admiration. To grainy photographs in are-you-going-to-buy-it-or-just-read-it newsagents. To our adolescence, when J.P.R., with his hair and sideburns, cooler even than Keef, danced through defences to the music playing in our heads. And we wish we too could live our lives like the Baa-Baas play. And since who we are is also where we've been and what we've seen, although our blood is yellow and blue, Barbarian F.C. is tattooed on our hearts.

Everyone's team

There are only a few truly mythical teams. And only one is unconditionally loved for its insouciant, devil may care, 'run it from our five-metre line' approach. Only one team consistently reminds us that, at one level at least, it's only a game and that we who watch it are all the same. If Man is God afraid, this team comes together and becomes divine. It's the spirit of the past, revisiting the present to weave its magic on the pitch, for pure love of the game. And when a player wears this shirt, he is ours forever.

They said what?

"It's not real rugby of course … nobody plays like that!" Springboks supporter to a friend at Twickenham in 2007 after the Baa-Baas had beaten their team 22–5.

"So how come they just did?" His friend's disgruntled reply.

"This is real rugby!" Lorenzo watching Baa-Baas' passing game.

"Have they got a place in the modern game?" Journalists after Baa-Baas' 14–17 defeat by England in 2008.

"This is why rugby needs the Barbarians." Journalists after the Barbarians' 25–18 victory over the All Blacks in 2009.

"I like three sports: Rugby Union, Rugby League and Barbarians Rugby." Betta in Crociati beer tent in 2011.

A night at the opera

The marketing men today speak about 'enhancing your match day experience' (ho! ho!) — a concept totally alien to our routine relationship with the stadium. Watching Crociati or Aironi is simply our bread and butter connection to the game — an attempt to feed a hunger and maintain well-balanced lives. It's just a part of us. But for Betta and me watching the Baa-Baas is doing something special — like going to the opera or riding a Ducati. It is 'a match day experience'. Though we're not going to sit in the dark with our eyes closed after the game if they lose.

Thank you, Mr Ellis

The Baa-Baas summer tour is an eight-day bubble of magic in our lives when we travel to Twickenham, then Dublin or Cardiff, or wherever they're playing this time, to watch an ever-changing mix of old and new players.

It's a celebration of spontaneity, a breaking out of the box, a climbing of mountains because they are there — a melting pot of players and supporters of different nationalities paying homage to their love of the game.

It's tradition and transience rolled into one. A hundred and eighty years of history blazing brightly for a few short days to burn into our memories.

The past is home

So are the Barbarians as great today as they were in the past? Of course they are! Same team, same greatness. Today's Baa-Baas don't simply exist in a bubble of time. It's what they did in the past that makes them what they are today. The past isn't a foreign country — it's the only country and it leads right into the present. Today's Barbarians are as good as they used to be, because they are their history. It's the same great ship, sailing down a river of time since 1890. It's just that the crew and the passengers have changed.

No place like home

But we need the past to be better because it's the myths of the past that give us our foundations in the present. And we want those foundations to be strong. So the Baa-Baas' victory over South Africa in 2007 won't stand up to scrutiny when set beside the 1973 game against New Zealand. And Visser's try against England in 2011 can't be compared to Gareth Edwards' dive into the left-hand corner at Cardiff Arms Park all those years ago.

So nothing will ever equal 'that game' and nothing will better 'that try'. Because we need it not to.

Saluting the Football Crowd

The football tribe

They're our cousins. But theirs is a more desperate hunger. We navigate a sea of emotions. But they ride a storm of feeling so intense, they break into another world — of manic bliss, and spiteful glee, and anger. Where we would be elated, they burn in fires of ecstasy. Where we are disappointed, they feel deep despair. We're buffeted by feelings. They surrender to the beast. For us, it's just a way of life; for them a measure of their existence. We marvel at their fever, from the safety of our confines. For we could never cross that great divide.

Another stage

We generally don't give a hoot about any round-ball-kicking team — it's not what beats our drum. But we sometimes take a passing interest, often when there's nothing else on television. And some of us actually go to a couple of matches a year. If we're all rugbyed up, it's a quick way of clearing our minds. But sometimes it truly is 'the beautiful game', and we can relate to the supporters when we're there. Because we know what they're feeling. From our own experience or — when they're really flying past Jupiter — from their expressions. Edvard Munch couldn't do it justice.

The artists

But they can do it justice. And they do. And maybe that's the point. Because they're the artists. The chosen few who explore a world where colours are brighter and emotions stronger. The people who break through the barriers of convention to punch you in the face (metaphorically speaking) with their creations. This is human joy, taken to the nth degree! This one's naked loathing! And this one's suicidal grief. And this is the song that a thousand souls should sing in unison. And we will bare our souls and dance before you if that's what it takes to touch you.

Performers one and all

And the players play their part. Expecting them to consistently defer to authority like respectful employees who fulfill their roles dutifully with professionalism and dignity, and know their place, is missing the point. Their place is at the centre of the show, reacting to the art of the stands, dancing to the tune called by their twelfth man.

So a football match is a journey inside an explosion of intense emotions. And varied too. Because sometimes the players add their own melodies to the music in the stands, as the beautiful game breaks out on the field.

So here's to them!

So long life to the footie fan and his world! A fascinating place to visit though we don't know if we'd want to live there. Or not for very long, anyway. But each to his own. And we've more in common with them than some of us would like to admit.

I think of them as part of the family. Sort of. Like those relatives you talk about with real affection and like to meet up with because they're a good laugh, but who you're not sure about inviting to your parties because you never know how the evening will end.

Gianni

Gianni wears the shirt of his football club with pride. Despite the odd-shaped ball they play with, he's not so different from us. He always wears the shirt, though it's very rarely visible. He's wearing it when he's working on a breast cancer project and when he's watching ducks take off on a lake against a tropical sunset. And he's wearing it when he lies awake at night, contemplating his own mortality.

Adriano

What draws Adriano to the stadium every fortnight is more about being than seeing. Being part of the spectacle — the spectacle of emotion. Being part of a pulsating mass of people on a journey of suspense that spontaneously ignites when a goal is scored, or just as suddenly implodes.

It's more about feeling than seeing. Feeling one with the crowd. Feeling events on the pitch through the cries and movements of those around him. Feeling a goal rush up through the ground.

For Adriano it's not about winning, but wanting to win.

Richard

Richard's been to hundreds of football matches though, for
reasons best known to himself, he stopped going ten years ago and
now follows a rugby club. He still feels attached to the team he
used to support, speaks to the guys he went with and looks for
their results. He didn't go to their playoff at Wembley since he
thought it'd be cheating. He says that if you don't do the donkey
work — the away games against small clubs on rainy Friday
evenings — you don't deserve to bathe in the glory at the glamour
matches.

Only one United

Joey's parents are Geordies but he's not, since his family moved down south shortly after he was born. But he still supports Newcastle United. His grandfather travelled to London for the 1955 Cup Final when they beat Manchester City 3–1. Joey's mother says he was shaking for weeks afterwards, buttonholing passers-by and giving them a minute-by-minute rundown of the match. He was shaking again eleven years later when he did the same for Joey and kick-started a love affair that's lasted nearly half a century.

Joey and Proust

Joey remembers sitting on a swing in his garden when he was a child and poring over his treasured programmes from the few Newcastle matches his father could take him to. He can still give you a rundown of the 1969 Fairs Cup winning side: *"McFaul, Craig, Clark, Gibb, Burton, Moncur, Scott, Robson ..."* And by now, so can we.

Since he moved to Italy he only sees them on TV and doesn't go to football matches. He comes to 6 Nations rugby games with us and sniffs the programmes — the smell evokes memories of his childhood match days, and more innocent times.

The greatest football team … the world has ever seen

Joey thinks that he was seen as a bit of a weirdo when he was at University in London in the late Seventies, because he was the only one of his circle who went to football matches. The Toon were in the second division at the time — the old English second level — and he used to wear his Newcastle scarf at college. He remembers feeling frustrated when an attractive young woman said "Trust you to support a marginal team!" and he couldn't make her understand that they were at the centre of the sporting universe.

Roberto

In May 1972, at home in Bologna, he watched a Scottish football team in blue shirts play a match on television and his future unfolded, unravelled, reshaped. He saw a light and walked towards it and he never looked back. He travelled to Ibrox Stadium several years later, the first of many pilgrimages in a life that would revolve around the Rangers fixture list.

They've brought him his closest friends and many of his greatest joys and sorrows. And his words of gentle, understated passion shroud us in blue and make us feel as if we too are Rangers fans.

One world

A mutual friend told him to look Roberto up if he was going to Bologna, because "he's a great Rangers supporter too". The friend went to see him thinking he'd simply meet "some Italian who says he likes Rangers and watches them on TV from time to time". He discovered that Roberto knew the name of nearly every player who'd ever worn the blue shirt they both adored, knew the result of every match in the last forty years and flew out to Ibrox four or five times a season.

When he got back to Glasgow he told his father about Roberto. And his father cried.

A chance meeting

Betta and I spend our summers in the Algarve in Portugal.
Portugal's one of those countries where association football seems
to be the national sporting obsession to the near-exclusion of
everything else. But we sometimes go to a couple of football
matches to try to alleviate the withdrawal symptoms generated by
our absence from rugby stadiums.

And so it is that after the 2010–11 rugby season — while still
looking for something to cling on to in the void left by our rugby
team's demise, while trying to understand where, if anywhere,
Aironi or Crociati fit into our lives — we stumble into Olhanense
Football Club.

Sporting Clube Olhanense

"Olha ... who?" I hear you ask. Olhanense! The football team from Olhão, population 42,000, on the south-west coast of Portugal, who currently lay claim to being 'the pride of the Algarve' since they're the only top-flight team in the region where, as in the rest of the country, nearly everyone supports Sporting, Benfica or Porto. They're into their third consecutive season in the Primeira Liga after a thirty-three-year absence. And with home-game crowds of under 4,000 and a mere 1.4 million euro annual budget — less than a tenth of the top-flight average — their main challenge must simply be to stay up another year.

The haves and the have-nots

The big three — Sport Lisboa e Benfica, Sporting Clube De Portugal and Futebol Clube Do Porto — are celestial bodies inhabiting their own private universe with annual budgets, crowds and prospects simply beyond the reach of the remaining thirteen top flight teams who, in competitive terms at least, just make up the numbers. Since the inception of the Primeira Liga in 1934 only two other clubs have won the championship — once in 1946 and again in 2001. The Big Three's budgets extend from 40 million to 95 million euros and their average crowds last season ranged from 27,000 to 40,000.

Not getting it

We don't usually watch football. It fills us with a sense of weariness and it irritates us when players go down and roll around in apparent agony because an opponent's breathed on them. And we don't like what we see as a lack of sporting behaviour from a large minority of the fans. If an opposing player's badly injured we're concerned for him. We hope he's all right and we'll applaud him as he's stretchered off the pitch. We'd never shriek out "Hope you die!" or make comments on his ability or parentage. We presume that the players know about their wives' sexual preferences and don't need to be informed by us. And the blanket of shrill whistling every time the opposition's got possession … we just don't get it.

Off the straight and narrow

But we're stadium people, as well as being rugby people. And during our annual holiday in the Algarve in Portugal, where the only sport on offer seems to be football, Betta and I start to twitch, like Italians after three days abroad without pizzas or pasta, and need to go somewhere there are crowds and floodlights. So we went to a couple of Olhanense games last year: a pre-season friendly against Nottingham Forest where the beer and good-humoured banter flowed freely between the two sets of supporters, and the championship's opener against a team whose name we can't remember.

Taking the diversion

And that — allied to the emptiness we still feel when we think of
Rugby Parma — is enough to pull us into the Sporting Clube
Olhanense merchandising stand at the Olhão Seafood Festival,
where few of the hundreds passing seem to be stopping. There are
three players in attendance, autographing the merchandise, and
we're struck by the care they take in signing the Olhanense baseball
cap we buy. "A hug and a kiss for Jack and Betta," they write
beside their names, as they tell us they're playing Sporting in
Lisbon at the weekend.

Taking a plunge

We'd heard about the Olhanense Expat Supporters Group with its members from Britain, Ireland, the Channel Islands and Belgium, so we look them up and get in touch. And yes, they're going to the Sporting match in Lisbon and, yes, there's room on the coach. Leaving Saturday 10am and returning in the early hours of Sunday morning. Forty-six euros for the 360-mile round trip, match ticket and lunch in Setubal. It sounds mad enough to us, but Betta's on dog-sitting duty so I go alone. She could do with the break anyway.

Lunch in Setubal

The coach doors hiss open and its cargo spills out onto the parking lot, to be kissed by a bright sun shining through a clear blue sky. Some, drugged up to the eyeballs with Olhanense and anticipation, glide smilingly into the restaurant on automatic pilot, ready to break into song and fill this sparsely populated corner of Setubal with the spirit of their team. Others group around the restaurant doors for pre-lunch cigarettes. A young woman in front of me, shining as brightly as the sun in her red and white shirt, turns to ask me for a light. And life feels good.

Inside the outer limits

For the next two and a half hours, they — or we — turn the restaurant into an anarchic wall of sound, veering from semi-melodious one-hundred decibel choruses and laughter to desperate eye-bulging oaths of loyalty to the Algarve team, as the restaurant staff flow impassively among gyrating dancers and upraised glasses. Normality's been put on hold, though it seems neither to deter others from coming in to eat nor to disturb the rest of the clientele present — some of whom take an 'if you can't beat 'em' approach and join in by clapping. Scenes like these are being played out all over Europe at this moment — and I'm lucky enough to be here.

Olha-nen-se! Olha-nen-se!

They'll take all this energy and hope and desire into sector A09 of the José Alvalade Stadium in Lisbon, forming part of an army of 800 or so away supporters, a small, desperate beacon of encouragement burning brightly for their team through a hostile crowd of over 32,000. And from the twenty-ninth minute, when Olhanense score first, against the run of play, they'll be craving the sound of the final whistle. And even though Sporting will dominate throughout and equalize in the seventy-seventh minute, the expected deluge will never come because — today at least — the Olhanense supporters will keep the skies clear through the power of prayer.

Crossing the encampments

As we'd entered Lisbon, we'd driven through groups of fans in Sporting colours eating and drinking at tables set up outside. They'd looked very much like Springboks rugby fans at their pre-match braaie. Some had gestured for us to stop and join them. Others had waved or indicated 3–0 or 4–0 with their hands. And who could blame them, given their budget and crowds and the quality of their team? But, hey … this is sport and anything can happen. And today it will.

The road back home

On the way out of Lisbon several Sporting supporters enthusiastically shake their green and white scarves at our coach and smile and wave at us, though three hooligan types lean dangerously out of their car, making angry gestures, and one of them throws a coin in our direction.

When we stop at the services for snacks at midnight the Olhanense President is there to shake the travelling supporters' hands and I'm introduced to him as a *novo adepto* — a new supporter. I'm not really, of course, though Betta and I will no doubt continue to go to their matches when we're over here on holiday.

Antipathy and distance

Football supporters … my head tells me I admire and respect their diversity but my heart just won't. We feel a slight antipathy towards football — perhaps the thing that smaller nations like Scotland, Wales or Ireland feel towards the all-pervading, overbearing presence of their larger neighbour England.

So I wasn't in Lisbon as a football fan but as part of a group of passionate people with Algarve on their backs, who were carrying their culture and their region northwards and who welcomed me into the fold and treated me as if we'd always known one another. As perhaps we had.

An attack on the immune system

You grow up with them — the sporting myths, the big brand names. And you can't quite get it out of you. And even if you don't really like football, it can still take your breath away when a team like Sporting Clube De Portugal runs out onto the pitch in front of a 32,000-strong cheering, baying home crowd. You can find yourself dragged along in the wake of mass emotion, whisked into a cauldron of intense feeling, wishing you belonged.

I was struggling against the tide, trying to keep a firm footing. Then Olhanense appeared before us, saluting their small band of travelling faithful, and the spell of the big time was broken.

Supporters for courses

It takes all sorts to make a world and there are many different types of supporters. Manchester United have 190 million supporters — or maybe they're just fans — in Asia, though what they have in common with a team from the north of England or the Greater Manchester community is hard to fathom. They've got 300 million supporters (or 'fans') worldwide. Including my sister. Apparently. Though she's never been to a match. An awful lot of people. And respect to them and good fortune.

But they're not our people. Our people sit in the stands at Old Trafford. Or the Moletolo stadium in Parma. Our people were all around me in section A09 of the José Alvalade Stadium in Lisbon on Saturday.

Epilogue

Epilogue

So what's it all about? I can't really tell you. If you stand on a stadium's steps each week, following the team you've always followed, you already know. And if you don't, you probably never will, although hopefully this book has taken you part of the way. It could never take you all the way, though. That I know, because I know what we felt before our ties to our club were cut and we went spinning off into space.

This book's called *This Is What We Are* but if I'd just been writing about our small group of supporters — the ones whose yellow and blue blood haemorrhaged all over the stadium floor — I'd have called it *The way we were*. Because for many of us I don't suppose there's any way back. But that doesn't mean we're no longer like you. Just that our circumstances have changed.

Epitaph — Game over!

Kicked out of play

The news came through like a bolt from the blue. It lunged at us from an Italian Rugby Federation press release on 6th April 2012. It was short, financial and to the point. Time is money, after all.

They weren't renewing Aironi's franchise licence for next season's RaboDirect PRO12 (the new name for the Magners League). Candidates to replace them had until 25/4 to register interest.

"Thanks and goodbye!" That's how it sounded to us. Well, apart from the thanks. There was no mention of the players, the staff or the supporters. I looked all over for some other announcement, but there was nothing.

Emotional investment, unwavering loyalty, a sense of community and commitment — these things have their place of course, but not in a profit and loss account.

We were there for the first game, the first long-awaited victory, the seemingly endless defeats, never getting off the bottom of the table but refusing to give up hope.

And now that hope's been crushed. In a few hours or less. That's all it takes for a handful of honourable men good and true to plunge a pen into the hearts of several thousand rugby people, destroying their dreams. It was done and dusted by 4pm on Friday, just in time for an early start to the long Easter weekend. All in an afternoon's work.

So Claudia, who's not going to give up, and Federica who can't bear it, and the rest of the four thousand who'll be packing the stadium this Sunday afternoon in solidarity and protest will all lose their team.

Our team.

Because Aironi Rugby is now set to disappear at the end of the season — as no doubt, too, will most of their supporters. But there'll be a new product for the punters to purchase. A new "match-day experience" dressed up in the words of our sport: Respect, Courage, Loyalty and Fair Play!

Words come cheap.

And they're not enough.

Living in a broken world

The death rattles sounded for 45 long days. The supporters congregated in their thousands for the last two games of the season, waving white hankies of hope not surrender from the stand, sharing food together and cheering the team desperately, as if the intensity of emotion pouring onto the pitch might change their destiny. Feel the force and let us live! Their banners pleaded respectfully and courteously to the President of the Federation, who stayed away: "Think again, Giancarlo!" No-one answered. In keeping with the values of our game, they stayed humble and polite.

We found others on social media and got together with them at the stadium. They weren't just people who went to the same games as us, but brothers and sisters in arms we simply hadn't met before, with whom we were now united in denial and stupor and driven forward together by faint glimmers of hope.

We made new friends abroad, as members of the global rugby family tweeted us messages of sympathy and support.

Aironi Rugby were going to take legal action and we clung to this for a while. Then they weren't. The Lombardy Regional Council, who had invested €4 million in the ground — our ground, yes ours — pushed for a meeting with the franchise and the Federation to try to thrash out a solution. Rugby Viadana, the main Aironi stakeholder, proposed soldiering on alone, without its former partners. The Federation agreed to consider their proposal. If they deemed Viadana's business plan sufficiently robust, we'd keep our team.

We'd keep our team. Our team now. We were cautiously optimistic, though the realisation that the efforts of our lads on the field and our voices in the stands seemed to count for so little when push came to shove was fairly humbling. If we'd seen a simple message of regret, however insincere, on the part of the powers that be, it might not have changed anything, but it would have been something.

There was another meeting on Saturday 19th March. The Federation rejected Rugby Viadana's proposal without possibility of appeal. And Aironi Rugby were consigned — not to the dustbin of history — but to a place forever in our hearts. Because the team may no longer exist on the field. But it'll live on. Because we were the team and we are the team. And we'll always be Aironi Rugby now. And Enrico and Gianni and Federica and Giulia and Claudia, and all the others we've met since the whole sorry story began, will always be our brothers and our sisters. And if there's an earthquake, or an accident on the motorway in the north of Italy, the tweets go out, from Bologna to Milan: are you okay? We are with you.

And whenever we meet in years to come, by accident or design, there will always be that bond between us. Because we'll know. Because we are the people. And Aironi Rugby and their players won't be forgotten.

But who will remember the men in suits?

Not us. We can't respect what they've done — their game. It's not the game we lived and breathed with Aironi.

For more information about this book, its author, his blogs and the opportunity to have your own say, visit:

Website: www.thisiswhatweare.com
Blog: www.parmajack.blogspot.com
Twitter: @Parma_Jack
Facebook: www.facebook.com/jack.fenwick.10

www.ingramcontent.com/pod-product-compliance
Lightning Source LLC
Chambersburg PA
CBHW031830090426

42741CB00005B/191